HUMAN RELATIONS

and

CORRECTIONS

FIFTH EDITION

Michael Braswell
East Tennessee State University

Larry Miller
East Tennessee State University

Donald Cabana
University of Southern Mississippi

WAVELAND

PRESS, INC.

Long Grove, Illinois

To
Tyler Fletcher

For information about this book, contact:
  Waveland Press, Inc.
  4180 IL Route 83, Suite 101
  Long Grove, IL 60047-9580
  (847) 634-0081
  info@waveland.com
  www.waveland.com

Contents

v

Section III
The Inmate   65

Section IV
The Correctional Officer   93

Section V
The Counselor   119

Contents

Section VI
Correctional Ethics 149

Section VII
The Correctional Administrator 183

Foreword

In film and on television, corrections is often portrayed primarily as an environment in which wardens, correctional officers and inmates interact—often violently. In truth, corrections is much more complex than that. While wardens do serve as the administrative head of prisons and correctional officers attempt to maintain custody of the inmates incarcerated there, many other criminal justice professionals and civilians also contribute to the life and times of offenders. Judges sentence offenders, probation officers supervise them in the community, and correctional counselors and caseworkers provide treatment interventions. Educational specialists attempt to teach inmates basic education skills, while vocational instructors try to impart marketable trades to their incarcerated charges. Chaplains and clerics of all faiths conduct religious services and provide valuable pastoral counseling to inmate populations.

In community settings, offenders are sentenced to traditional probation as well as alternative programs in such areas as substance abuse and juvenile boot camps. Recent community correctional and justice innovations such as restorative justice programs are also on the increase. These kinds of programs may include victims of crime, the offender, criminal justice professionals, family, and other affected members of a given community in interventions. Of course, when inmates have completed their sentences or are paroled, they typically return to the communities from whence they came and find that they need a number of support services for adjustment purposes.

Human Relations and Corrections allows the reader to identify with various roles involved in the correctional process. The roles of inmate, judge, probation officer, correctional officer, counselor, and warden/superintendent are representative of critical relationships that enhance or detract from the rehabilitative and correctional potential of incarcerated offenders. Understanding and gaining insight into these and other roles can help an individual to relate more effectively to the offender, professional peers, and the community in general. It is the authors' contention that effective relationships are the major contributors to correctional successes, no matter what the setting. This book allows the reader to analyze real-life situations that are a part of the correctional process. As with all life situations, the solutions to the case studies presented are not usually black and white, but are more often gray. Each choice or option comes with a cost.

A number of new cases have been added to this edition, including topics covering religion and correctional treatment, privatized community corrections, death row, correctional officer/inmate relations, inmate suicide, and politics and corrections.

All names and scenarios portrayed in this book are fictitious. Any similarities the cases may have to any real persons or situations are strictly coincidental.

ACKNOWLEDGMENTS

We want to thank the students and colleagues in academic and agency settings who have provided valuable input regarding suggestions for case topics and other ways of improving this book.

We are particularly indebted to Dan Moeser for his tireless efforts. Finally, we would like to thank our editor, Gayle Zawilla, for her efforts and support.

Michael Braswell
Larry Miller
Donald Cabana

The Court and Corrections

The courts have a greater impact on corrections than perhaps any other component of the criminal justice system. Whether dealing with the civil rights of prison inmates or abused children, courts represent whatever parity that is to be found in our system of justice. In the next eight cases and text you will encounter problems from the viewpoint of court professionals. As a family court judge you will have to use your judicial discretion concerning a child-abuse case. Other cases require deciding the appropriate purpose and limits of a presentence investigation and determining the consequences for a repeat juvenile offender.

INTRODUCTION

The criminal and appellate courts are, in a sense, the hub of the criminal justice system around which all the other components revolve. The court system is highly structured, authoritative, and dictated by laws and tradition (Neubauer, 1979). The remainder of the criminal justice system depends upon and is usually subservient to the courts. Police procedures are governed by court decisions regarding arrests, search and seizure, interpretation of existing statutes, and the definition of legal case decisions. The correctional system also looks to the courts for its charges as well as program guidance. Correctional laws affecting civil rights of prisoners, right to treatment, methods of treatment, and institutional procedures have come largely from case law decisions of higher courts (Feeley, 1979).

Criminal court cases are often viewed as melodramatic episodes or contests between two opposing forces vying to prove the technical guilt or innocence of a defendant (Pound, 1929; Samaha, 1997). Prosecutors usually take a stand before the jury that attempts to portray disgust of the evil that the defendant allegedly committed. Prosecutors may attempt to encourage the jury to look upon the defendant in contempt and as a destructive individual needing punishment. Defense attorneys usually make a play for the jury's "heart" in attempting to show that the defendant is a victim of society, an abusive family environment, or the harassment of law enforcement officials. In some cases, the defense may also attempt to make the jury angry that the defendant was "railroaded" or set up by the accusers. The judge may be seen in this instance as a referee making decisions on motions and testimony. Judges usually try to weigh all the consequences of a decision. If a judge makes a wrong decision, it will more than likely be questioned in the appeal process.

Juries are composed of "lay" individuals who usually know little about the criminal justice system (Miller, 1984; Ellsworth, 1989). Most of their experiences with court procedures are the result of media representations of court cases in fiction or in news broadcasts. Attorneys for both the prosecution and the defense will try to use the juror's lack of knowledge to their advantage in presenting their case (Ellsworth, 1989). For many court cases involving jury decisions, the finding of guilt or innocence often appears to be due primarily to personalities rather than facts at issue (Chambliss and Seidman, 1982; Ellsworth, 1989; Hastie, Penrod and Pennington, 1983).

A basic concept of the American criminal justice system weights the scales of justice toward the freedom of an offender rather than risk the conviction of an innocent person. The only requirement in finding an accused individual not guilty is a reasonable doubt. However, a reasonable doubt is difficult to define, and what may be reasonable to one may be unreasonable to another. Therefore, court procedures which protect the rights of the accused are usually observed "to the letter" (Kagehiro, 1990).

Our laws have always allowed for the incarceration of serious violent offenders and discretionary options of incarceration and probation for other felonies. Over the last quarter of the twentieth century, concern increased over the number and frequency of violent crime. Legislators, in order to appease their constituencies, supported mandatory sentencing and incarceration for a number of serious offenses. The result of these laws and concerns is that in most states the penalties for criminal violence have increased, while provisions for parole and other remissions of sentences have decreased or been limited. While it is debatable whether these laws have accomplished desired goals, they are certainly filling up and overcrowding our correctional institutions (Quinn, 2003; Cole and Call, 1992). In response to this reality, judges and correctional personnel have focused more heavily on nonviolent offenders for sentencing alternatives.

PRESENTENCE DIVERSION

In the past, a judge had relatively simple choices for sentencing convicted offenders. If the defendant was found guilty, the sentence was prescribed by law in the form of time spent in prison. However, judges must now choose from a broad range of judicial alternatives, particularly when the offender is nonviolent. These alternatives include electronic house arrest, pretrial diversion, shock probation, day reporting, restitution, restorative justice programs, and a wide range of other options. In states where the jury may also set the sentence, they, too, have found that a number of options are open for their deliberation, some which can be very confusing (Blumstein, 1983).

In deciding a sentence, the duration of a sentence, or whether to place an offender on probation, a judge may utilize a presentence investigation report. A presentence investigation is generally prepared by a probation officer, court officer, or social worker. The presentence investigation report includes information about the convicted offender that assists the judge in making a sentencing decision. Such a report might include information regarding the present offense and previous offenses, the offender's attitude toward the offense, family history, educational history, occupational history, habits (e.g., alcohol and drug usage, gambling, etc.), and the

offender's physical and mental health. The report is usually concluded with summaries and recommendations (Jones, 2004;
Schwartz and Travis, 1997). Table 1 illustrates a typical presentence
investigation report format. Presentence investigation reports vary
widely among states and local jurisdictions, but most contain the
information illustrated in table 1.

Probation is among the most widely used sentencing alternatives. It is derivative of the suspended sentence. The suspended sentence differs from probation because it does not require the offender
to be under supervision, and usually does not prescribe a specified

Table 1   Presentence Investigation Information Chart

A. Personal Statistics
1. Name (include nickname or aliases)
2. Address
3. Telephone
4. Age, Place, Date of Birth
5. Sex, Race, Social Security Number
6. Marital Status
7. Children and/or Family Information
8. Physical Health
9. Mental Health
10. Social History (character, attitude)
11. Education
12. Employment History

B. Offense Statistics
1. Offense(s)
2. Docket No. and Court
3. Judge
4. Defense Counsel
5. Prosecuting Attorney
6. Plea
7. Penalty for Offense(s)
8. Referrals
9. Custody Status
10. Co-Defendants and Dispositions
11. Detainers or Charges Pending
12. Previous Convictions and Dispositions (rap sheet)
13. F.B.I. Number
14. Mitigating and Aggravating Circumstances
15. Official Police Version of Offense
16. Defendant's Version of Offense
17. Recommendations
18. Probation Officer/Investigating Officer

set of goals for the offender to work toward. Probation is actually a form of sentence in itself (Quinn, 2003). The probationer must be supervised by a probation officer, follow strict rules, and in some cases attend counseling sessions with probation or other treatment professionals. Community service and restitution may also be a part of the considerations of probation. Judges may impose a wide array of "conditions of probation" which an offender must comply with, or face the likelihood of incarceration. One of the most important advantages of probation to a community is that probation is much more economical than incarceration. Many individuals may view probation as a "slap on the wrist" for an offender. However, the major purpose of probation is not to punish, but to treat and provide guidance for the offender. Offenders placed on probation should be those who are of low risk to the community and have the potential to become law-abiding citizens.

Probation is not an appropriate option for the "hard-core" and violent criminal whose incarceration is primarily for the protection of the community.

There are basically two forms of probation: (1) probation with adjudication, and (2) probation without adjudication. In probation with adjudication, the judge finds a suspect guilty of an offense and then places him or her on probation. With non-adjudicated probation, the judge withholds sentencing until the offender has successfully completed a probationary period. If the offender is successful on probation, the judge may dismiss the case. One of the most common forms of non-adjudicated probation is the first offender program.

First offender programs usually allow an arrested individual to be placed on supervised probation before sentencing. If the first-time offender successfully completes the probationary period and treatment, the outstanding charges against the individual are dismissed by the court. With this program, the offender receives no criminal record because there is no conviction. This allows the offender to have a "second chance." First offender programs have been shown to be an effective probation device for local communities (Liberton, Sliverman, and Blount, 1992).

JUVENILE COURTS

The juvenile court differs for each state and in some instances, within states. The juvenile court is a special statutory court enacted by local and/or state legislation. Only a few states currently have a statewide juvenile justice system. Juvenile courts are usually controlled by a municipality and/or county government. The philosophy of the juvenile court is to care for, protect, and reform juveniles. Traditionally, the juvenile court has not been viewed as a court of punishment, although current trends appear to indicate that it may be becoming more like the adult system.

Because of the traditional philosophy toward juvenile offenders, the terminology used in juvenile court varies from adult court. For instance, juvenile offenders do not commit crimes, they commit delinquent acts. If a juvenile commits a crime by statutes (delinquent act), he or she is served with a petition and attachment rather than an arrest warrant. In most cases, a juvenile is considered to be legally incapable of committing a crime. A juvenile offender cannot be charged or indicted, but a petition and attachment can be issued against them. Because of the non-criminal approach to juvenile offenders, many of the due process rights of adult offenders have been omitted from juvenile court procedures (Rudman et al., 1986; Feld, 1993). The informality of the juvenile court prevailed for over sixty years. Many individuals held to the care-and-protection philosophy of the original juvenile court and justified its practices on grounds that actions were taken only for the benefit of the child (Feld, 1993). Since the Gault decision in 1967, juvenile courts have generally applied due process rights to juvenile offenders. Table 2 illustrates the major due process court decisions since the late 1960s.

In addition to juvenile offenders, the juvenile court has jurisdiction over many other juvenile matters. Status offenders (e.g., children in need of supervision) are juveniles who have not committed an offense for which an adult could be prosecuted (e.g., possession of alcohol or tobacco, playing gaming machines, curfew violations, running away, etc.). The juvenile court, or in some cases the family court, may also have presiding jurisdiction over child-abuse cases, divorce settlements involving children, and other civil matters involving children. The juvenile court may have primary or shared jurisdiction with adult courts over adult offenders. The juvenile court needs to have some influence over adults whose acts, encouragement, indifference, or indulgence are often the major cause of a child's problem. For this reason, jurisdiction over adults who contribute to the delinquency or dependency of children has been vested in the juvenile courts of many states. The juvenile court may also have jurisdiction in cases involving children and adults. These situations include truancy, guardianship, child labor law violations, non-support and desertion, paternity suits, and adoptions. In some jurisdictions, these courts may also be referred to as family courts rather than juvenile courts.

Table 2 Major Court Decisions Affecting Due Process Rights for Juveniles

Date	Court Case Citation	Court Decision
1966	Kent v. U.S., 383 U.S. 541	Juveniles must be given a hearing in juvenile court that must "measure up to the essentials of due process and fair treatment," before being tried as an adult offender.
1967	In re Gault, 387 U.S. 1	Juveniles in juvenile court have the right to counsel, right to remain silent, right to cross-examination and con-frontation of witnesses against them, and the "essentials of due process and fair treatment."
1970	In re Winship, 397 U.S. 358	Determination of delinquency may only be made on the same standard for evidence in criminal proceedings. "Proof beyond a reasonable doubt" replaced the old juvenile court standard of "a preponderance of the evidence."
1971	McKeiver v. Pennsylvania, 403 U.S. 528	The right to jury trials in juvenile court was considered by the U.S. Supreme Court but was not granted.
1975	Breed v. Jones, 421 U.S. 519	Juveniles are protected against double jeopardy by the Fifth Amendment. A child cannot be adjudicated in juve-nile court then transferred to an adult court to be tried on the same offense.
1979	Smith v. Daily Mail Publishing, 443 U.S. 97	As long as information is legally obtained, a state cannot restrict a newspaper from publishing a juvenile offender's name unless the restriction serves a substantial state interest.
2005	Roper v. Simmons, 03-633	Juveniles who commit capital offenses while under the age of 18 are pro-tected from the death penalty.

DIVERSIONARY PRACTICES

The concept and meaning of diversion is often confusing. Some use the term interchangeably with prevention, police discretion, or efforts to minimize an offender's involvement into the criminal justice system. Diversion emphasizes informal, administrative decision making to determine: (1) if nonjudicial processing is warranted; (2) if a particular offender requires treatment and, if so, the type of treatment; and (3) if the charges against an offender should be dropped or reinstated. It is assumed, under diversion, that such decisions are more individualized and treatment oriented than within the formal due process justice complex (McDonald, 1985).

Despite the courts' growing use of diversionary programs, such a trend is not without opposition, especially in the juvenile arena. Critics view this practice as potentially harmful. The term "net widening" has become a popular refrain with critics of diversionary programs, who caution that while such programs may be well intended, their ultimate effect is to pull juveniles even deeper into the criminal justice system. They maintain that: (1) this practice often promotes diversion to other programs rather than from the system; (2) some of the goals of diversion are generally unattainable (e.g., informal procedures, eliminating label stigma, etc.); and (3) most formal diversion practices are not in accordance with due process rights for adults and juveniles (Sigler and Lamb, 1995).

In the 1990s, with dramatic increases in various categories of juvenile crimes, many states enacted laws that made it easier to try juveniles as adults, for certain violent offenses. As a result, although many questions have been raised about the appropriateness and effectiveness of various diversionary programs, it seems unlikely that the use of diversion will decline in the future (O'Leary, 1984; Morgan, 1994). The increasing numbers of court cases and offenders in correctional institutions, and the fact that many offenders are divertable, support the increased use of diversionary programs and its anticipated endurance. Nearly half of all arrests are probably divertable. Although few serious violent crimes in which weapons are used may be diverted, many misdemeanor offenses may be handled appropriately outside the criminal justice system.

As prison overcrowding continues to increase, legislators and correctional administrators have sought innovative correctional methods to reduce inmate populations. Various reform efforts have included forms of alternative sentencing for nonviolent offenders (Klein, 1988) and intermediate sanctions, such as intensive probation, house arrest, and electronic monitoring (Smykla and Selke, 1995). In addition, the practice of shock incarceration for adult and juvenile offenders in the form of military-model boot camps and wilderness experiences have been instituted in a number of states (Jones, 2004; MacKenzie and Shaw, 1990).

The perceptions and assessments of these diversionary practices are mixed. Some researchers have voiced skepticism about the utility of such programs (Morash and Rucker, 1990; MacKenzie, 1990), while others have indicated positive views (Osler, 1991; MacKenzie, Gould, Riechers and Shaw, 1989). Despite the criticisms of such programs, public opinion tends to support such diversionary programs. They do appear to save money and reduce prison populations and also appear to appease the public demand that judges and correctional officials "do something" rather than simply put an offender on probation (Quinn, 2003; Morash and Rucker, 1990).

Summary

The courts are the hub of the criminal justice system around which law enforcement and corrections revolve. Procedures for law enforcement and methods for corrections have largely come as a result of statutes, cases, and constitutional law interpretations of higher courts.

Because of a broad range of judicial alternatives to sentencing of criminal offenders, many judges rely on presentence investigation reports on offenders. Such reports assist judges in determining sentence, probation, or treatment.

Many courts are resorting to formalized diversionary practices for convicted offenders. Probation has become the most popular form of diversion. Other forms of diversionary programs (e.g., first offender programs) have shown success in offender treatment and decreasing recidivism rates.

Juvenile courts have a tremendous impact on the criminal justice system. Although the juvenile justice system is a separate system, law enforcement, corrections, and judicial decisions are reflected in the juvenile courts' role and responsibilities. The juvenile court may have jurisdiction in adult cases involving contribution to the delinquency and dependency of minors, family conflicts, civil cases involving children, and child abuse. Since the late 1960s, juvenile courts have established due process rights for juvenile offenders. This incorporates the juvenile court into the justice system, which is important to the procedures and methods in which law enforcement officials and correctional officials handle juvenile problems.

The courts have a tremendous impact on the criminal justice system as a whole and the correctional component in particular. The courts decide whether an offender is to be institutionalized or placed on probation. Probation and diversionary programs are used with increasing frequency in the courts. This creates new responsibilities for correctional workers. It conceives a need for increased counseling contacts and incorporates the community into the helping role for offenders. These alternative practices have shown promising results in terms of success rates. Still, critics maintain that the courts' use of such diversionary practices may be improperly interpreted and in some cases result in a violation of due process rights. Nevertheless, such diversionary programs seem to be a positive step toward a much needed reevaluation of the correctional process.

References

American Correctional Association. (1994). *Field officer resource guide.* Washington, DC: ACA.

Blumstein, A. (1983). *Research on sentencing: The search for reform.* Washington, DC: National Academy Press.

Chambliss, W. J. and Seidman, R. B. (1982). *Law, order, and power,* 2nd ed. Reading, MA: Addison-Wesley.

Clear, T., Clear, V., and Burrell, W. (1989). *Offender assessment and evaluation: The presentence investigation report.* Cincinnati: Anderson Publishing Co.

Cole, R. B. and Call, J. E. (1992). When courts find jail and prison overcrowding unconstitutional. *Federal Probation* 56(1):29–39.

Conrad, J. P. (1985). The penal dilemma and its emerging solution. *Crime and Delinquency,* 31:411–22.

Ellsworth, P. C. (1989). Are twelve heads better than one? *Law and Contemporary Problems* 52:205–24.

Feeley, M. (1979). *The process is the punishment: Handling cases in a lower criminal court.* New York: Russell Sage Foundation.

Feld, B. (1993). Juvenile (in) justice and the criminal court alternative. *Crime and Delinquency* 39(4):403–24.

In re Gault. (1967). 387 U.S. 1, S.Ct.

Hastie, R., Penrod, S. D., and Pennington, N. (1983). *Inside the jury.* Cambridge, MA: Harvard University Press.

Jones, M. (2004). *Community corrections.* Prospect Heights, IL: Waveland Press.

Kagehiro, D. K. (1990). Defining the standard of proof in jury instructions. *Psc Sc* 1:194–200.

Klein, A. R. (1988). *Alternative sentencing: A practitioner's guide.* Cincinnati: Anderson Publishing Co.

Liberton, M., Sliverman, M. and Blount, W. (1992). Predicting probation success for the first time offender. *International Journal of Offender Therapy and Comparative Criminology* 36(4):335–47.

Littrell, W. B. (1979). *Bureaucratic justice: Police, prosecutors, and plea bargaining.* Beverly Hills: Sage Publications.

MacKenzie, D. (1990). Boot camp prisons: Components, evaluations, and empirical issues. *Federal Probation* 54(3):44–52.

MacKenzie, D., Gould, L., Riechers, L. and Shaw, J. (1989). Shock incarceration: Rehabilitation or retribution? *Journal of Offender Counseling, Services and Rehabilitation* 14(2):25–40.

MacKenzie, D. and Shaw, J. (1990). Inmate adjustment and change during shock incarceration: The impact of correctional boot camp programs. *Justice Quarterly* 7(1):125–47.

Morash, M. and Rucker, L. (1990). A critical look at the idea of boot camp as a correctional reform. *Crime and Delinquency* 36(2):204–22.

McDonald, W. F. (1985). *Plea bargaining: Critical issues and common practices.* Washington, DC: National Institute of Justice.

Miller, L. S. (1984). Juror's perceptions of the criminal court system. *Criminal Justice Review,* 10:11–16.

Morgan, K. (1994). Factors associated with probation outcome. *Journal of Criminal Justice* 22(4):341–53.

Neubauer, D. (1979). *America's courts and the criminal justice system.* Scituate, MA: Duxbury.

O'Leary, V. (1984). Criminal sentencing: Trends and tribulations. *Criminal Law Bulletin,* 20:417–29.

Osler, M. W. (1991). Shock incarceration: Hard realities and real possibilities. *Federal Probation* 55(1):34–42.

Palmer, T. B. and Lewis, R. V. (1980). A differential approach to juvenile diversion. *Journal of Research on Crime and Delinquency,* 17(2):209–22.

Pound, Roscoe. (1929). *Criminal justice in America.* New York: Holt, Rinehart and Winston.

Quinn, J. F. (2003). *Corrections: A concise introduction,* 2nd ed. Long Grove, IL: Waveland Press.

Reckless, W. C. (1967). *The crime problem,* 4th ed. New York: Appleton-Century-Crofts.

Rosett, A. and Cressey, D. (1976). *Justice by consent: Plea bargains in the American courthouse.* New York: Lippincott.

Rudman, C., et al. (1986). Violent youth in adult court: Process and punishment. *Crime and Delinquency,* 32(1):75–96.

Samaha, J. (1997). *Criminal justice.* St. Paul, MN: West Publishing Co.

Schwartz, M. D. and Travis, L. F. (1997). *Corrections: An issues approach.* Cincinnati: Anderson Publishing Co.

Sigler, R. and Lamb, D. (1995). Community-based alternatives to prison: How the public and court personnel view them. *Federal Probation* 59(2):3–9.

Smykla, J. and Selke, W. (1995). *Intermediate sanctions: Sentencing in the 1990s.* Cincinnati: Anderson Publishing Co.

Presentence Investigation
A Fair Shake?

The case was a shocking revelation to the community when the arrest was made by the state bureau of criminal investigation. The sheriff had not even been aware that an investigation was under way, much less that such a prominent citizen as Johnny James was involved.

As you follow the trial, it becomes apparent that you will be given the presentence investigation. The outcome of the trial has never seemed to be in doubt. Public indignation that a former state's attorney should be involved in receiving stolen property and disposing of it in conspiracy with a convicted felon was high. The stolen items, worth tens of thousands of dollars each, included heavy equipment that had been stolen from construction sites, stashed out on the attorney's ranch, and ultimately disposed of through a third party. It was a lucrative racket and probably would have gone undetected had not one of the buyers offered to sell a bulldozer back to the same contractor from whom it was stolen. The rightful owner quickly identified the bulldozer by an unusual mechanical modification that had been made before the equipment was stolen from a roadside work site. The resultant investigation revealed altered serial numbers and criminal intent.

You know that the presentence investigation is going to be tough. There are those who may soften their criticism because of current associations with Johnny James, and those who may want to "hang" him because they believe a public official, even an ex-public official, ought to set a moral example in the community and certainly not be a common "fence" for stolen goods.

The investigation progresses quickly and Johnny James is now out on bail. James had been a fine high school athlete, president of his class, and had attended the best law school in the state. He soon established himself as a smart lawyer and an ambitious and success-ful businessperson. Fifteen years later, he now owns a controlling interest in a farm implement company, a thriving automobile busi-ness, and an interest in a large motel. He is considered a friend of law enforcement, hosting a large annual party for area law officers. He is also a model member of the community in most respects, with strong church affiliations and membership in several respected and prestigious civic organizations. His wife heads a local hospital volun-teer effort, and there is no indication of any rift within the family. Aside from strong contrasting opinions of local citizens, there is no indication of danger to citizens if this particular offender continues to reside in the community.

However, one matter bothers you about this investigation. Why should this "big time" lawyer who was involved in the theft of thou-sands of dollars worth of private property be out on bail? He may never even serve one day of "hard time," while an ordinary thief would no doubt receive a more traditional sentence in the state pen-itentiary. You feel that crime is crime, whether white collar or not.

You wonder if you should look deeper into Johnny James' back-ground for indications of a pattern that might predict continued crim-inal behavior. Perhaps his campaign contributions and his political connections should also be investigated. You know for a fact that his motel is frequented by out-of-town prostitutes who are never arrested. This kind of information could influence the judge and might even result in a prison sentence.

Questions for Discussion

Regarding the case of Johnny James, you are painfully and some-what angrily aware of the different qualities of justice available to offenders according to their means. The question lingers: "Why should James have a better chance for judicial consideration than a more common thief?" On the other hand, although his crime was quite serious, up until this offense Johnny James had apparently led a productive life well within legal boundaries. Should you, as the pre-sentence investigator, dig deeper into James' past or limit your que-ries to the specific case with which he is involved? What are the rehabilitation prospects for this particular offender?

Diversion or Subversion?

You pore over the presentence evaluation: two intoxicated college females, one DUI and the other trying to run from police officers, both with no prior arrests, and both nursing majors at the local college. As judge, you must decide whether to sentence them to probation or place them in a diversion program. Further complicating your options, you have to choose between a private probation agency (Accelerated Diversion, Inc.) and the state's probation diversion program. The private agency appears to be very progressive and boasts an impressive array of alcohol and drug education, counseling, and follow-up services, while the state agency's services seem to be more traditional and limited. In addition, the attorney representing the two students indicated they would prefer to be referred to Accelerated Diversion, Inc.

You have been a judge for ten years and you take your job seriously. It would be easy to accede to the young women's wishes, yet you find yourself becoming increasingly uneasy about what you are hearing through the grapevine about Accelerated Diversion. At worst, the rumors suggest that Accelerated Diversion is nothing more than a fee collection agency, where probation officers' salaries are largely dictated by commissions they receive from fees they collect. Accelerated Diversion's critics contend that probation officers spend very little time with their clients, and what appears impressive on paper is for the most part nonexistent in practice. You do know for a fact that the executive director of Accelerated Diversion makes $80,000 a year, which is twice what other comparable agency directors make in your city. Still, their clients, who are for the most part middle class, seem pleased with their services. In addition, the state department of probation has a fairly limited approach to alcohol and drug diversion, and they do not appear to be very interested in any new or creative approaches. Yet you have known the people who have worked there for a long time. They are solid and dedicated, if overworked, correc-tions professionals. What would be best for the two young women? Which agency would have the greatest impact on them?

Questions for Discussion

Do you, as the judge, have any other options you can think of? Should you allow your personal beliefs about the private agency to interfere with your sentence? What recommendations do you think the presentence investigators would make? What recommendations do you think the district attorney would make? How should private agencies be controlled and/or monitored to insure they are providing the services they should?

The Court and Child Abuse

As a lawyer you always enjoyed private practice. However, after ten years of successful practice, you decided to enter public service and politics. You and your family realized that public service does not have the financial rewards of a private practice, but your ten-year law practice solidified your financial situation. Over the years you have made some important personal connections and a good name for yourself. On your first attempt at public service, you were elected county prosecutor. Being a prosecutor was a different kind of law practice: your new job was to convict people in the name of the state, instead of defending them. Of the variety of cases you prose-cuted, some naturally stirred your interests and working capacity more than others. Because you are a family man, the crime of child abuse was one of the crimes that always seemed to make you press harder. You always attempted to prosecute abusive parents to the full extent of the law and have their children removed to a non-threaten-ing environment. Trials for this offense always proved to be an emo-tional experience for you.

Your career as county prosecutor progressed rapidly. Eventually you were appointed a family court judge, a position which again proved to be a different world. You now have to evaluate facts objec-tively, rather than approach the case primarily from a prosecutor's or defense lawyer's point of view. Your first case of child abuse as judge proves to be a very difficult experience. The family is very prominent in the community. Both husband and wife are successful profession-als, highly regarded by their colleagues. The police discovered the abuse as a result of a family disturbance call. The abuse had appar-ently been taking place for a short time, and because of the family's community standing it had been covered up. The abuse seemed to have resulted from marital problems which had led both parents to heavy drinking. During an argument between the couple, their seven-year-old son interrupted them. From then on they focused and projected their problems onto the child. The actual physical abuse was usually a belt strap across the back of the young boy. The psychological damage to the youth as a result of his parents' behavior was, of course, impossible to measure. You are also troubled by another subtle aspect of this particular case. Apparently, the child in question spends most of the time when he is not in school with a variety of sitters, typically seeing his parents for one or two hours each night. He also frequently spends his weekends with grandparents.

You are not the county prosecutor or defense attorney now. You are the judge, and you must try to do what is best for all concerned, especially the boy. Should you take him out of his home? If you do, you will be taking him away from the place he lives and from his natural parents. His parents are in a financial position to do a great deal for their son, whereas a government agency could not. More important, the boy does love his parents and seems to want to stay with them. On the other hand, if you do not remove him from the home, he could be subjected to even more severe abuse. Hopefully, the court experience might open the eyes of the parents to their need for professional help in solving their problems and child-abuse tendencies, but there is no way to be sure. Do you take the child out of his home, or do you let the parents keep custody and hope that the child will not be subjected to further abuse?

Questions for Discussion

In this particular case, you must think of the parents as well as the abused child. Could family counseling and psychotherapy rehabilitate the parents in this instance? If you should decide on this course of action, what specific recommendations should you make regarding the family's treatment program? Do the parents need to rethink their priorities?

CASE 4

Probation or Prison?

You could have been in the same situation yourself. Instead, it is Mary Lee Smith, one of your probationers, who is about to stand before the judge in a probation revocation hearing.

When you and your husband split ten years ago, you had two children and eventually had to declare bankruptcy and accept food stamps in order to pay the rent. After seven years working as a secretary at the nearby state juvenile corrections center, receiving constant encouragement from Mrs. Jones, the superintendent, and taking advantage of a criminal justice scholarship program, you finished a degree in administration of justice and qualified for an entry-level position with the community resources division of the state department of corrections. You advanced as the system grew and now, three years later, you are a probation supervisor in Judge Longworth's court.

In a way, Mary Lee is as much a victim as she is an offender. Married at seventeen, she quit high school and moved west with her serviceman husband. By the time she was twenty she had two children and was divorced. With babysitters to pay and skills that would command no more than minimum wage, Mary Lee turned to such income supplements as shoplifting, bad check writing, and occasionally prostitution. Her check-passing skills developed rapidly, and it was not long before she had amassed a series of convictions, not to mention several lesser offenses for petty larceny which were disposed of by the prosecutor's declaration of *nolle prosequi* (a formal entry on the record by the prosecuting attorney that he will not prosecute the case further). To date, Mary Lee has not served a day in prison. Admonition, restitution, suspended sentence, and probation have all been used by Judge Longworth in efforts to rehabilitate Mary Lee. However, Mary Lee's criminal conduct has persisted, as has her inability to stretch her food stamps, welfare payments, and part-time

19

minimum-wage employment into a satisfactory existence for herself and her children. To make matters worse—or better, according to whoever you happened to be talking to—the welfare safety net that had helped keep Mary Lee and her children afloat would cease to exist for her within 24 months.

Judge Longworth has called you into his chambers before the hearing. He read your violation report with interest. You pointed out Mary Lee's family obligations and the imminent possibility that the children would have to be placed in foster homes if she is confined. You also pointed out that she has been faithful in making restitution and that she maintains a regular church relationship and a satisfactory home environment for her children. Although your report is fair and accurate, you realize that the judge has sensed your own misgivings and uncertainty concerning Mary Lee.

Judge Longworth looks up from your report and comes directly to the point. "Do you really believe this woman deserves to go back into the community? You certainly seem to have found some redeeming features in her conduct that I don't," he says. "Unfortunately, it appears to me that the only way she is going to learn to respect other people's property is to be deprived of her own freedom. I think the community is getting pretty tired of this kind of repetitive criminal conduct." With that, Judge Longworth looks to you expectantly for your opinion.

You are on the spot. You know your answer might put Mary Lee in the penitentiary or give her another chance on probation. The judge will make up his own mind, but you know he values your opinion.

Questions for Discussion

Should Mary Lee be sent to prison or allowed to remain on probation? Is there anything else you can do as a probation officer to help Mary Lee make a more successful adjustment regarding living within the limits of the law? How might the new, limited welfare system affect Mary Lee Smith and her children?

CASE 5

Child Rapist

You are an assistant district attorney in a small circuit court region. The region consists of three counties with an average population of 80,000 people per county. The community you serve is primarily composed of middle-class people with middle-class values. Having come from a large city, you are particularly impressed with the small-town atmosphere and easy way of life.

The district attorney general hired you straight out of law school two years ago. You felt that a job with the D.A.'s office would be an excellent opportunity to gain needed experience and develop a reputation as a good lawyer. Your ambition is to enter the political arena and perhaps run for state representative in a couple of years. You have stressed a "law and order" image in order to accomplish your career ambitions.

As you prepare to look over the court docket for tomorrow's cases, your secretary advises you that Sheriff's Investigator John Wainwright is waiting to see you.

"John, come in. I was going to call you about our burglary case tomorrow. You didn't have to come over here in person today."

"Thanks, Bill, but I need to talk with you about another matter. You know, we arrested a young man by the name of Fred Granger a couple of days ago for rape and I wanted to fill you in on some details," the investigator begins.

"Yes, I was at the arraignment, remember?" you respond jokingly.

Fred Granger is a twenty-two-year-old white male who works in a nearby factory. He has a high school education and no prior felony arrests or convictions, but he does have a previous conviction for DUI two years ago and one for possession of marijuana three years ago. He has been charged with the rape of a 13-year-old girl under state code 37–1–2702:

> Any adult who carnally knows a child under the age of fourteen
> by sexual intercourse shall be guilty of the capital offense of rape.
> The punishment for same shall be not less than ten years nor
> more than thirty years in the state penitentiary without parole. It
> shall be no defense that the child consented to the act or that the
> defendant was ignorant of the age of the child.

The punishment for this offense is no different than for the crime of forcible rape in your state. Fred Granger was arrested on a complaint from the parents of a thirteen-year-old girl named Debbie. It seems Fred picked Debbie up for a date, went to the lake, and had sexual intercourse with her. It was a clear violation of the law and an apparently easy conviction, since Fred admitted to arresting officers that he had sex with Debbie.

"So, what information do you have for me, John?" you ask.

"We've obtained statements from everyone involved. This is basically what went down. Fred knew Debbie's sister, Nina, who is twenty years old. Fred and Nina had gone out before on a couple of dates in the past and have had intercourse. It seems Nina and her younger sister, Debbie, have the reputation of being 'easy.' Anyway, Fred called Nina for a date and Nina wasn't at home. Debbie answered the phone and started flirting with Fred. Fred asked Debbie if she wanted to go with him to the lake and Debbie agreed. Debbie apparently wore a very revealing bathing suit and 'came on' to Fred. They had intercourse and Fred dropped Debbie back home. Debbie's parents inquired about her activities for the day and Debbie told them everything, even about the sex. That's when we got the call. Fred states that he thought Debbie was over eighteen and that Debbie consented to having sex with him. Debbie supports this story. Both of them were drinking beer at the lake," said the investigator.

"Yes, well, I see. But, it's no defense for Fred to be ignorant of her actual age and no defense for him that Debbie consented. He probably got her drunk anyway. The law is clear on this matter," you advise.

"Yes, I know. But this Debbie has a reputation of being very promiscuous. She is very open about the fact that she consented. She now says she's in love with Fred. Needless to say, her parents aren't very happy about her attitude, but they seem to have very little control over her or her sister. Besides, anyone who's seen Debbie could make a mistake about her age." The investigator pulls out and shows you a recent photograph of Debbie.

The photograph surprises you. You had never seen the victim, but in the photograph Debbie looks well over twenty years old.

"Hey, she does look at least twenty," you respond. "She certainly would have fooled me."

"Yeah. Anyone might assume that," the investigator replies.

Looking over the statements that the investigator brought, you begin to feel uneasy about the case. In a legal sense, Fred is a criminal. He violated the state law. He has no legal defense. The girl is under fourteen, which means she cannot testify that she consented. The fact that she has had intercourse before also cannot be used as a defense for Fred. It seems to be an open-and-shut case. Fred is looking at ten to thirty years with no chance of parole. Even if he got the minimum ten years, it is still a stiff punishment for ignorance. You decide to call on the district attorney general for advice.

"Yes, Bill. I see why you are concerned. It seems to me you have three options here. One, you could *nolle prosequi* the case. Two, you could reduce charges through a plea bargain arrangement. Or, three, you could prosecute to the fullest extent of the law. It's basically a choice between legal ethics and personal ethics. Legal ethics would dictate that you prosecute to the fullest. A crime by statutes has been committed and you are sworn to uphold the law. In that sense, it would not be legally ethical for you to *nolle prosequi* or plea bargain when you have such a strong case. And, if you did, it might affect your political career. The news media and the public would not take your letting a 'child rapist' off without comment. On the other hand, your personal ethics dictate that this Fred fellow is not a typical criminal. He's guilty of stupidity, maybe. But, apparently when you look at Debbie, you can see why. If you prosecuted the case, the jury might see Debbie the way Fred saw her and acquit him. But that is a big chance to take. Juries are unpredictable and you can't bring up the fact that she 'looks' of age. I don't know, Bill. It's your decision. I'll back you on whatever you decide."

Questions for Discussion

How would the community and justice be served by prosecuting this case? How could the correctional system "rehabilitate" Fred; or for that matter, help Debbie? Do you think the jury would nullify the law by acquitting Fred? What legal defenses does Fred have? What would be the consequences of *nolle prosequi* or plea bargaining? What do you think would happen with Fred if he was found guilty and received ten years without chance of parole?

CASE 6

The Court and Wife Battering

You are a court caseworker en route to a home visit on a spousal assault probation case. Six weeks ago Terrance O'Dell was arrested for wife battering. Ms. O'Dell called police to "stop her husband from hurting her." The result was a mandatory thirty days jail time and one year probation. Although Ms. O'Dell did not testify at court, the responding officer's testimony was sufficient. In your state, the victim of spousal abuse does not have to press charges if the police have sufficient probable cause to believe an assault took place. In this case, Ms. O'Dell's swollen face and bloody nose were sufficient enough for the police to arrest Mr. O'Dell.

Mr. O'Dell has just been released from the county jail and is back home with his wife and two small children. You are required to make periodic home visits to determine if the rules of probation are being followed and the victim is not endangered again. As you pull up to the O'Dells' residence you note that while the house is obviously in a low-income neighborhood, it is neat and well kept.

Ms. O'Dell comes to the door.

"Hello, Ms. Roberts. Please come in and have a seat." Ms. O'Dell politely invites you in.

"Is Mr. O'Dell here?" you ask, looking around the small living room area.

"Here I am. I was out back changin' oil in the car. Sorry I might be a little dirty."

"That's alright. As I said on the phone, I just wanted to stop by to check to see if everything was going smoothly since your release." You fumble through your attaché case, looking for the case file.

"Everything's just fine now, isn't it honey?" Mr. O'Dell hugs his wife around the shoulders.

"Oh yes. All is well now, thank you," Ms. O'Dell replies a little nervously.

"Let's see now, Mr. O'Dell. The court has ordered that you undergo alcohol counseling at the Alcohol and Drug Treatment Center. When is your next appointment there?"

"Why, I was there yesterday to check in after my release. Had to fill out some papers and stuff. I'm supposed to see my counselor next Thursday," Mr. O'Dell responds.

"So, how is the alcohol problem?"

"Haven't had a drop in over a month now. It was rough while I was in jail but I don't need it anymore, isn't that right honey?" Mr. O'Dell looks over toward his wife.

Ms. O'Dell smiles and nervously nods her head in the affirmative.

"Mr. O'Dell, would you mind if I talked with your wife in private, please?"

"No, no, not at all. I've got to finish up on the car outside. But she'll tell you everything's just fine now," Mr. O'Dell pats his wife on the shoulder as he leaves.

"Now, Ms. O'Dell. How are things . . . really?"

"Just like he said. Everything's fine now," she responds nervously.

"Doesn't sound like you are too sure."

"Well, to be honest with you, he did get a little drunk yesterday after he got out, but he was under a lot of stress. He lost his job at the truck company because he was in jail so long. But he might be able to get on at this construction company next week."

"Did he assault you or threaten to hurt you in any manner when he got drunk?" you inquire.

"Well . . . no, not really. He fussed a lot. But he's got a right to, you know. It was my fault that he got in jail and lost his job. I should have never called the police. But, at the time, I was afraid for the kids, you know?"

"Yes, I think I do. You know that if he threatens you or the children we can have him locked up again. You don't have to put up with this," you advise.

"No, no. I wouldn't want that. We can't afford him to go back to jail. Like he said last night, if he went back, me and the kids would have nothin', no money, no food, nothin'. We couldn't live without him to support us," Ms. O'Dell states.

As you leave the O'Dell's house you cannot help but feel uneasy about the situation. It appears to you that the time Mr. O'Dell spent in jail was not particularly helpful for his problem or his family. As you walk to your car, you notice a neighbor washing his car next door.

"Excuse me, sir. I'm Officer Jane Roberts with court services. I wonder if I could ask you about your neighbors, the O'Dells?" You show your credentials.

"Are you going to put that asshole back in jail? I came close to calling the cops last night after I seen him curse poor Mrs. O'Dell on the front porch. That guy's dangerous. If I was her I'd shoot him, especially when he starts on the kids," the neighbor states angrily.

You realize now that the problem is still present in the O'Dell household. You have the power to revoke Mr. O'Dell's probation with probable cause. However, maybe it would be best to wait to see if the alcohol counseling and probation will do any good. Still, if you wait until it is too late. . . .

Questions for Discussion

How long should you wait to see if things really do get better in the O'Dell household? Do you think revoking probation would do any good? What if you waited and Ms. O'Dell or the children were seriously hurt—would you be liable? What are the advantages and disadvantages of mandatory arrest and jail time for spousal assault cases?

Juvenile Probation
Boot Camp or Boot Hill?

"Your honor, I know I've done wrong . . . more than once . . . but I know I can do right, if you will just give me one more chance with Ms. Simpson, my probation officer. I couldn't take boot camp. My nerves wouldn't stand it. Just ask my mother."

"He's right, Judge Arnett," Tony's mother quickly responded. "Dr. Platt, our family psychiatrist, has indicated in Tony's file that he couldn't withstand the rigors of such an experience." Getting teary-eyed, she continued, "You will also note in the report that Tony's brother, Louis, committed suicide while at boot camp in the Marines. We thought the experience would straighten him out, but it was a terrible mistake. His death has put us all through a terrible ordeal and has made a lasting impression on Tony."

"That's right," Tony added, "I've never been the same since my brother died."

Scanning Tony's social history, you locate the psychiatrist's report and find that Tony's mother's responses are essentially accurate. You also note that Ms. Simpson's comments suggest that Tony is highly manipulative, especially concerning his mother's and father's feelings of guilt regarding his brother's death. In addition, you note that this is the seventeen-year-old's third and most serious offense, breaking and entering.

You are considering two basic sentencing options. You could sentence Tony to two years at the juvenile training school or give him the option of attending the 90-day juvenile boot camp. You could also extend his traditional probation sentence.

It seems evident to you that Tony has benefitted little from psychiatric counseling. In fact, his parents probably need such services more than he does. It is equally apparent to you that Tony isn't a particularly stable individual and probably is, to some extent, affected by his brother's death.

There is another option, but one that is much more expensive. An Outward Bound program is operating near the national forest which has one staff member for every five students. Its success rate has been as impressive as its price tag. Boot camp is politically popular, but you are not very impressed with the long-term results. Within six months of their graduation from boot camp, you have seen many of the same young men standing before you in court with new offenses. And, finally, you know in your "heart of hearts" that Tony would not last long physically or emotionally in the juvenile training school.

It is time to render your decision. You must balance what is in Tony's best interest with needs of the community. Is Outward Bound really worth the expense? Boot camp has helped a lot of young men, but is it for everyone? More importantly, is it for Tony?

Questions for Discussion

Tony needs structure and discipline; boot camp can give him that. Tony is also unstable. Would boot camp be too damaging to him psychologically? Should the cost of a program like Outward Bound be the factor determining whether or not a juvenile offender is referred to it? Are there other alternatives that you can identify that will help Tony and/or reduce the costs associated with the Outward Bound program?

Lost Boys, Inc.

It says it right there on your letterhead—"Judge Sharon W. Elliott, Juvenile Court, Fourth District." For the last seven years, you have done what you could to give the troubled youth of your district all the help you could find within the limits of the law. The single mother of a teenage daughter and grown son, you know how hard it is to keep boys and girls positively motivated and out of trouble. You want to judge wisely, humanely and fairly, but sometimes, as in the case before you, there is no clear answer.

Joey Martinez is a fifteen-year-old boy appearing before you for the second time. He's more of a nuisance than a danger to the community. Like many a young man with a bit of a chip on his shoulder, Joey wants to be noticed and seeks attention in inappropriate ways. You placed him on probation a year ago with a six-week stint in a drug education program for public intoxication and selling a small amount of marijuana. This time around, Joey was caught breaking windows at the local high school with two older boys. His probation officer has also informed you that he suspects Joey has also participated in a local teen-age shoplifting ring that merchants are complaining about. Joey's dad is a single parent trying to raise Joey and his younger sister on a librarian's income.

Your choice seems simple enough. Lost Boys, Inc., a highly touted program of The Institute of Character Development, has been recommended to you by Joey's probation officer. You have made a few calls and while there is no solid empirical evidence, anecdotal accounts by a number of parents and the school principal suggest that the program may be a good fit for Joey. Unfortunately, Joey's dad doesn't agree and wants Joey to be placed on traditional probation again. Ed Martinez, who considers himself an agnostic, believes adamantly in the separation of church and state and doesn't want his son participating in a program he considers little more than a recruiting program for Christianity. You have talked with Reverend Bobby Joe Simpson and checked his credentials. While it is true he doesn't have an academic degree in psychology or mental health, his seminary education did include some courses on pastoral counseling. Reverend Simpson claims his program is not religious but is more in keeping with the current "restorative justice" movement. Still, you can understand Mr. Martinez's concerns after reading the Lost Boys brochure. The character development training includes concepts of confessing one's wrongdoings; making some form of restitution; seeking forgiveness from those one has wronged; and experiencing redemption through confession, restitution, and a new attitude of service to others. One other feature that troubles Mr. Martinez is the footnote at the bottom of the brochure indicating that "while not required, religious and social support services are available to young men and women who request them."

You understand a parent's desire to raise his or her child according his or her own values. That said, this is the only option currently open to you besides traditional probation, and if Joey gets in trouble again, he could be sent to the regional juvenile prison. You will have to render your decision within the hour.

Questions for Discussion

How important should a parent's wishes be in a case like this? What might be some advantages and disadvantages in assigning Joey to the "character development" program? As a judge, you have limited choices. What should you do?

SECTION II

The Correctional Role
of the Community

Members of a community contribute to the quality of justice they experience. The following eight cases and text will allow you to relate to correctional situations from a variety of community perspectives. The school teacher who has a disruptive student, the minister who has a parishioner who is an ex-offender, and the community halfway house director all present possible solutions to correctional problems in their communities.

31

INTRODUCTION

Change and reform in the American criminal justice system is a slow process. The manner in which criminals are apprehended, tried, convicted, and corrected has remained virtually the same for nearly two centuries. New ideas of treatment for offenders are often impeded due to political pressure, economics, and societal attitudes. Community-based corrections is not a new idea. In 1967, the President's Commission on Law Enforcement and Administration of Justice acknowledged community-based corrections by indicating that prisons isolate offenders from society, which cuts them off from their families and supportive influences within the community (e.g., jobs, schools, etc.). Furthermore, such incarceration tends to label offenders as criminals in a permanent sense, decreasing their chances of successful reintegration into society (Kappeler and Potter, 2005). The concept of community-based corrections grew from three basic issues: (1) increased concern over prison conditions, (2) the rising cost of incarceration, and (3) belief in the efficacy of rehabilitative programs (Jones, 2004; Martinson, 1974).

THE COMMUNITY CORRECTIONS CONCEPT

Community-based corrections is a philosophical commitment to the humane and effective treatment of offenders. Community corrections provides, ideologically, for meaningful ties between offenders and their local environment. Community based programs afford offenders a much greater opportunity to maintain crucial family ties, and to benefit from other ties to a wide range of community services. These ties include education, recreation, food, banking, employment, religion, sanitation, mental health, and legal aid services. Previously, correctional programs have operated in out-of-sight-out-of-mind prisons and training schools. Even today, many community correctional programs operate in the same out-of-sight tradition despite their locations within a community (e.g., halfway houses, probation and parole). If a correctional program is located within a community, it is not necessarily community-based corrections. The mere operation of a group home or work-release center within the community is no guarantee that any meaningful ties with the local community will be developed (Chaneles, 1980).

MODELS OF COMMUNITY-BASED CORRECTIONS

Three basic models provide the foundation for community-based corrections: (1) diversion, (2) advocacy, and (3) reintegration (Smykla, 1981).

In addition to these three models, the Alternative Dispute Resolution (ADR) is an informal process that is used to settle disputes on issues between offenders and victims (Champion, 1996). Increasingly referred to as the Restorative Justice Model, this community-based approach is gaining popularity among prosecutors and victims rights advocates because it allows for the direct participation of both victim and offender. In such instances, restitution, rather than punishment, becomes the focus.

Diversion refers to the substitution of formal criminal justice proceedings against an offender with therapeutic training and/or educational programs. There is some confusion about the precise meaning of the term diversion. Some use the term interchangeably with crime prevention, police discretion, and efforts to minimize the involvement of an offender into the criminal justice system. The National Advisory Commission on Criminal Justice Standards and Goals (1973) defined diversion as "formally acknowledged and organized efforts to utilize alternatives to initial or continued processing into the justice system. To qualify as diversion, such efforts must be undertaken prior to adjudication and after a legally proscribed action has occurred."

Diversion programs may be characterized as conditional or unconditional. Those that remove the offender from the criminal justice process and place no conditions on his or her post-diversion behavior are unconditional diversion programs. Those that restrict the offender's post-diversion behavior, monitor his or her progress in the community, and provide for a reinstatement of prosecution if the conditions of the diversion are not met are conditional diversionary programs. Because these programs maintain the option of returning the offender to the criminal justice system for prosecution, they are sometimes referred to as deferred prosecution programs.

The philosophy of diversion emphasizes informal, administrative decision making in an effort to determine: (1) if nonjudicial processing is warranted, (2) if a particular offender needs treatment, (3) the type of treatment required, (4) if the selected treatment has been successful, and (5) if charges against the offender should be reinstated or dropped. Such decision making is often more desirable than formal court system decision making, since it is more individualized and treatment oriented. It is also less restricted by due process requirements of adjudication. Diversionary programs are concerned with the offender's problems and the needs of the community rather than determining offenses committed and punishments in a legal sense.

Diversionary programs may be classified by the stage of the criminal justice system at which the diversion occurs. Diversion programs that provide alternatives to the arrest of an individual are often referred to as police-discretion or arrest-stage programs. These programs may be administered by police agencies or by public or private organizations working closely with the police. Juvenile diversion programs are often administered by police agencies (Lemert, 1981). Diversion programs that focus on offenders who have been arrested but not convicted are typically referred to as pretrial diversion programs. In such cases, the prosecution usually makes the decision to divert an offender prior to filing criminal charges. Such decisions are made in the same manner as plea-bargaining agreements between the prosecution and defense. Over two hundred pretrial diversion programs are in operation today, and the number is increasing (Potter, 1981; McShane and Krause, 1995). The majority of these programs are administered by the district attorney's office, the court, the probation office, or the public defender's office; the remaining programs are operated by private or public noncriminal justice agencies (e.g., religious groups, etc.) (Austin and Krisberg, 1981; Schwartz and Travis, 1997).

Most pretrial diversion programs are conditional. Offenders are required to comply with certain stipulations, such as participating in a rehabilitative or treatment program. Over two-thirds of all programs require offenders to make victim restitution and/or perform community service (Potter, 1981). If the program is not successful, criminal charges may be reinstated against the offender. Some of the more common arrest-stage and pretrial diversion programs include alcohol detoxification centers, family crisis intervention units, programs for vocationally disadvantaged offenders, programs for juvenile offenders, programs for drug-abusers, and neighborhood justice centers.

The advocacy model for community-based corrections stresses the need for social change rather than offender change. Advocacy is designed to end arbitrary decision making through the institution of specific criminal justice, social services, and educational reforms at the state and local levels. Those in favor of advocacy stress the failure of existing correctional and community resources, and encourage the development of new resources for offender treatment within society. Advocacy focuses on community involvement for offender treatment and accountability and, as a result, it has encountered tremendous resistance in many communities.

The re-integration model is concerned with the reduction of crime by focusing on both the community and the offender. The

basic assumption is that offenders become offenders because of situations at home, in school, or in the community itself. The re-integration model attempts to involve the appropriate community service to
alleviate the offender's problems (e.g., vocational counseling and
training, school counseling, employment, etc.). It is important that
community re-integration programs include a high degree of interaction between the correctional program and the community's
resources. Community re-integration programs include halfway
houses, work-release, study-release, group homes, pre-release centers, and furloughs.

According to the U.S. Department of Justice, Bureau of Justice
Statistics, of the defendants who had state felony charges filed against
them in the nation's 75 most populous counties during May 2000:

- An estimated 62% were released by the court prior to the disposition of their case. Thirty-eight percent were detained until
  case disposition, including 7% who were denied bail.

- Released defendants were most likely to be released on com-
  mercial surety bond (37%) or their own recognizance (26%).

- Murder defendants (13%) were the least likely to be released
  prior to case disposition, followed by defendants whose most
  serious arrest charge was robbery (44%), motor vehicle theft
  (46%), burglary (49%), or rape (56%).

- Less than half of defendants with an active criminal justice status, such as parole (23%) or probation (41%), at the time of arrest
  were released, compared to 70% of these with no active status.

- About a third of released defendants were either rearrested for
  a new offense, failed to appear in court as scheduled, or committed some other violation that resulted in the revocation of
  their pretrial release.

- Of the 22% of released defendants who had a bench warrant
  issued for their arrest because they did not appear in court as
  scheduled, about a fourth, representing 6% of all released
  defendants, were still fugitives after 1 year.

- An estimated 16% of all released defendants were rearrested
  while awaiting disposition of their case. About three-fifths of
  these new arrests were for a felony.

THE ROLE OF THE COMMUNITY IN CORRECTIONS

The role of the community in correctional programs depends
largely on the interaction between the criminal justice system, politi-

cal influences, and public attitudes. Typically, citizens respond to criminal activity by demanding greater action from the police and courts. For nearly two decades, the police sector has been promoting the concept of crime prevention to the public. The police have attempted, with some success, to educate the public regarding their responsibility in crime prevention and control. The correctional sector has also attempted to relay to the public their responsibilities for treatment of offenders. Although this endeavor has not been promoted on as grand a scale as crime prevention programs, corrections has made progress in community efforts toward offender treatment. Citizen involvement in voluntary services, counseling centers, clinics, hotlines, vocational outreach, and so on are examples of these efforts (Jones, 2004).

The community has not always been viewed as comprising the answers to offender problems. For many years, the community was viewed only as harboring the causes of crime; "the evil influences of alcohol and bad company" were viewed as the principal sources of criminal behavior. Correctional institutions seemed to offer a relief from temptation; removed from a corrupting environment and placed in confinement, an offender could change his or her ways through penitence (hence the term penitentiary) (Latessa and Allen, 2003; Quinn, 2003). Many early community-based correctional efforts were criticized because they were contrary to the "reform through isolation" approach. It was believed that bringing ex-offenders together in halfway houses and group therapy was asking for trouble because they would inevitably revert to criminal behavior. It has taken many years to overcome this view of crime, criminals, and the community. In a number of areas it is still difficult to establish community corrections programs, such as furlough programs, because of such beliefs (Fischer, 1988).

PROBATION AND PAROLE

Probation is currently the most widely used post-conviction correctional program. It permits offenders to remain in the community while they receive counseling and assistance. Probation attempts to ensure community protection through the monitoring and supervision of offender behavior (Jones, 2004; Latessa and Allen, 2003; Schwartz and Travis, 1997). Probation differs from diversion programs in that the offender has been officially adjudicated. The granting of probation is a judicial decision. The sentencing judge grants probation after determining that an individual offender is suitable for community supervision. This judgment is reached by referring to statutory eligibility requirements and by assessing the offender's background, often by means of a presentence investigation report (Newman, 1978; Samaha, 1997; Latessa and Allen, 2003).

Probation supervision usually involves a synthesis of police and counseling activities. Because of large caseloads, probation officers may utilize the community to assess offender needs, refer offenders to appropriate agencies, and monitor their progress in the community. The conditions of probation serve both reform and control objectives. They reflect individual needs and capabilities as well as maintain control of the offender for community safety (Austin, 1981). If the conditions for probation are violated by the offender, or if the offender commits another criminal offense, the probation may be revoked and the offender may be incarcerated.

By the end of 2003 more than 4.8 million men and women were under probation or parole supervision on local, state, and federal levels (Bureau of Justice Statistics, 2004). Almost three times as many offenders are placed on probation each year as are sentenced to prison. Despite more punitive legislation initiatives for offenders, probation is increasingly becoming more and more popular as prison overcrowding worsens. Recent trends in sentencing indicate many judges prefer a combination of probation and prison such as split sentences, shock incarceration, and intermittent incarceration (e.g., weekend sentences).

Proponents of increased use of probation usually indicate that prison experiences actually increase recidivism among offenders. Petersilia and Turner (1986) reported that prisoners had a significantly higher recidivism rate than a matched group of felons on probation. Opponents of increased use of probation indicate that felony probationers pose higher risks to the community (Petersilia et al., 1985). Many states have adopted a more controlled form of intermediate sanction called intensive probation. Intensive probation allows for closer monitoring of offenders through surveillance, drug testing, home visits, electronic monitoring, and house arrest (Smykla and Selke, 1995).

Parole is the supervision of offenders granted release from prison by a parole board (Samaha, 1997; Quinn, 2003; Jones, 2004). It is an executive-branch decision rather than a judicial decision, as in the case of probation. Inmates may be released through the expiration of their sentence (flat-time) or upon the accumulation of "good-time" credits. Parole assumes that inmates may be released when incarceration has achieved its maximum benefit and that community-based guidance, counseling, and behavior monitoring will both assist the ex-offender in his or her attempt to avoid future crime and protect the community during the adjustment period. Most inmates are released on parole so that their behavior may be monitored in the community. Prison overcrowding is one factor that has encouraged an increase in the use of parole (Benekos and Merlo, 1992). There are three essential elements of parole: (1) preparing inmates for release and developing pre-parole reports for prisoners; (2) conducting hearings regarding parole eligibility, granting parole, and revoking parole and terminating parole supervision; and (3) supervising parolees in the community.

INNOVATIONS IN COMMUNITY CORRECTIONS

The 1970s witnessed phenomenal growth in community-based correctional programs. With federal assistance funds (e.g., LEAA), many communities funded programs that were poorly planned and/ or implemented. When research began to demonstrate that community-based correctional strategies were valuable but often not very effective, program growth began to slow. Political conservatism and the economic recession of the 1980s also contributed to the decline in program growth. However, the loss of much federal assistance and political and economic factors of the 1990s have resulted in attempts by many states and communities to develop innovative correctional programs. Victim restitution, community-service programs, volunteer groups, and house arrest are examples of innovative programs for community-based corrections.

Restitution and community-service programs are designed to restore what has been lost as a result of a crime. Monetary restitution programs provide financial payments from the offender to the crime victim. Community-service programs make restoration by requiring the offender to work in programs or on projects designed to enhance the public welfare (Schwartz and Travis, 1997; Jones, 2004; Whitehead et al., 2004). Although the concept of restitution has been around for centuries, it has played an insignificant part in the criminal justice system. Traditionally, the state or the people have been viewed as the injured party in a criminal offense. Community-service programs have been developed in an attempt to provide creative alternatives to monetary payments. Today, restitution and community-service programs are common alternatives or supplements to traditional dispositions, because they combine benefits to the offender, the victim, and the community.

Although restitution and community-service programs appear to be relatively simple responses to the crime problem, several legal and social issues have emerged with their use. The desirability of full versus partial payments for restitution, low-income or unemployed offenders' ability to make payments, the voluntariness of restitution agreements and their enforcement, amount of services required to pay back the community for certain offenses, net-widening, etc., have all been raised with restitution and community-service programs (Jones, 2004; Latessa and Allen, 2003; Quinn, 2003; Schwartz and Travis, 1997; Benekos and Merlo, 1992). In addition, some critics have argued that such programs are not punitive enough for a number of offenders (Tonry and Hamilton, 1995). Due to overcrowded prison and jail conditions, an offender might be sentenced to an intermediate sanction without regard to public safety or the ability of the program to benefit the offender. These issues should be systematically addressed in any program attempting to use restitution or community service before implementation. Despite these issues, restitution and community-service programs have achieved the support of the community and criminal justice practitioners on the basis of their economic benefits to the victim and service benefits to the community.

Citizen participation in corrections is essential for meaningful correctional benefits. Volunteer efforts have continually increased in support and popularity. The use of volunteers in community corrections permit criminal justice agencies to make better use of professional staff, individualize services to offenders, and increase public awareness of correctional programs, problems, and issues. While some improvement in the use of volunteer services is needed (Kratcoski, 1981), many states are exemplary in that they require volunteers to undergo the same training and qualifications as regular staff. Areas of improvement for volunteers in community corrections include recruitment, training, and government support. The drawbacks of volunteer services, however, do not hamper its usefulness in community corrections. Volunteers can also serve as role models for reform. In many volunteer programs, ex-offenders are used to help the client through adjustment difficulties and counseling (Carney, 1977). In many cases, an offender is more prone to take advice from one who has "been there before" (Reiff and Reissman, 1964). If properly used, volunteers can significantly improve the quality of community correctional programs.

As prison overcrowding worsened in the 1990s, the pressure to divert offenders to community-based alternatives increased. House arrest is a sentence imposed by the court in which the offenders are legally ordered to remain confined to their home. Over twenty states have adopted house arrest as an alternative to prison for nonviolent offenders. Electronic monitoring systems, usually in the form of a bracelet, are used to detect violators. While many feel that house arrest is an intermediate form of punishment that could bring relief to prison overcrowding, some critics maintain that such a program may result in ineffective rehabilitation and increased civil liberties intrusions (Berry, 1985; del Carmen and Vaughn, 1986; Smykla and Selke, 1995; Whitehead et al., 2004).

COMMUNITY ORGANIZATION FOR CORRECTIONS

The development and maintenance of a successful community corrections program relies on a balance between public attitudes, the criminal justice system, and related systems (i.e., education, employment, housing, etc.). Typically, when large bureaucratic systems such as the criminal justice system develop social programs to which the public is indifferent, problems arise. Attitudes are often indifferent to community corrections programs except when interest is aroused by a particular circumstance or incident.

Certainly, a community will ask several important questions when asked to undertake a community-based correctional program. Who or what group of individuals will administer, control, and direct the treatments and programs within the community? What types of offenders will be the recipients of such a program? What types of programs will be provided by the community, and at what cost?

Local control and administration of community correctional programs were shown ineffective in the total outcomes of correctional treatment. Record keeping, financial obligations, minimum treatment standards, fiscal and budgetary control, and local politics have been factors of failure for community corrections. State-level offices, which monitor community control of corrections, provide special services and records maintenance (that local communities may not possess), and still allow community control of basic operations and treatment programs; this seems to be the best approach to the problem (Latessa and Allen, 2003; Logan, 1990; Bowman and Elliston, 1988).

Concerning selection of recipient offenders and costs of the community programs, the community should probably be substantially left in control. The community is often best able to determine recipients from interviews, transcripts, and personal knowledge of the offender. State probation and parole agencies have not shown great success in predicting outcomes of offenders in correctional treatment programs. The community itself may be better suited to make such predictions and not jeopardize public safety by failing to incarcerate dangerous offenders. Costs should be under local control with monitoring at the state level. If the community is to actively participate in corrections, they should not work strictly from handouts of state and/or federal grant monies. The interested community should be encouraged to develop programs that are cost-effective and beneficial by reducing the likelihood of a return to criminality by one of their own community members.

JAIL: POLICE/CORRECTIONS INTERFACE

The law enforcement community appears to becoming more involved in the correctional process than has traditionally been the case. With the rising problem of prison overcrowding in state prison facilities, city and county jails are increasingly utilized as long-term correctional institutions. Prior to 1980, jail populations remained relatively stable. However, between 1988 and 2003, jail populations grew from a daily rate of 343,569 to 762,672 inmates—a 45% increase (Bureau of Justice Statistics, 2004). Much of the increase has been due to states using local jails to house state prisoners. Since 1988, the jail and prison population in the United States has increased more than six times to a staggering 2.1 million prisoners.

Many county and regional jail facilities are paid through state funds to house state prisoners. Such practices provide a number of benefits. First, the local community is provided additional revenues to house state prisoners. It is usually cost-effective to house one-hundred inmates as opposed to fifty since the increase of food and utility costs are only slightly higher. Second, the state prisons are allowed to combat overcrowding problems by allowing less serious offenders to serve their sentences in local jails. The state is able to reduce the costs of building new prison facilities which, in turn, saves tax money. Third, those state prisoners housed in local jails are usually assigned a jail in close proximity to their homes. This allows for more frequent visitation from family members and support from their own community. However, once the door to local jails was opened for state prisoner occupation, it has rarely been shut. The result has been serious overcrowding for local jails, diminished community safety, and a general failure of local jails to provide appropriate correctional treatment programs (Zupan, 1991; Kinkade, Leone and Semond, 1995).

The basic difference between a jail and a prison is that a prison utilizes correctional treatment programs and is intended for long-term incarceration, while a jail is intended to be used as a temporary detention center. With increasing intake of state prisoners housed in local jails, the jail can no longer be seen only as a temporary housing facility. Improved standards for local jails and personnel could provide more correctional responsibilities and alleviate more of the overcrowding in state prisons.

Traditionally, city and county jail personnel have been low-priority areas of law enforcement. A police officer working as a jailer was often either much older, physically inhibited from regular police duties, or serving punitive time for errors committed on the street. Fortunately, this is changing. Jail personnel are becoming better trained, and in some cases "certified" as correctional officers and counselors. Many states have legislated standards for local jail correctional personnel, as they have for police personnel. Some of these standards include: (1) separate job descriptions for officers working within jails (i.e., civilian vs. police personnel), (2) minimum entrance requirements and standards for new jail personnel, (3) mandatory basic jail personnel training, (4) mandatory annual in-service training, and (5) minimum program standards for services provided by jails (e.g., medical, treatment, physical plant, etc.).

Many jails have incorporated correctional treatment programs such as "work-release" and recreational programs formerly found only in prisons. Many sheriffs and local jail administrators viewed the constitutional rights of inmates which emerged in the 1960s and 1970s as confusing, burdensome, and frustrating. With the availability of state and federal funds to house state and federal prisoners, these same sheriffs and jail administrators are now able to provide services without the benefit of court decisions. Many counties have changed old "work-house" jail systems into contemporary "work-release" programs. Under work-release programs, selected inmates are released from the jail during the day to continue regular jobs in the community while spending daily after-work hours and weekends in confinement. Many jails are using the old "trustee" status for inmates as work-release inmates, thereby releasing many of them from such activities as cleaning the courthouse or washing police cars to gainful employment and/or skills development. Recreational and educational programs in local jails have decreased the number of inmate assaults and staff-inmate conflicts by providing an outlet for cell-block boredom. Community support and resource groups have contributed educational instruction and facilities (e.g., vocational school instruction, YMCA, church groups, etc.) as well as equipment to local jail inmates (e.g., weight lifting, ping-pong, video games, etc.).

SUMMARY

The concept of community-based corrections grew from three basic issues: (1) increased concern over prison conditions, (2) the rising cost of incarceration, and (3) belief in the efficacy of correctional treatment/rehabilitation. Community corrections provides meaningful ties between offenders and their local community. Traditionally, correctional programs have operated in out-of-sight prisons and training schools.

Three basic models have established the foundation for community-based corrections: (1) diversion, (2) advocacy, and (3) re-integration. Diversion has been the most widely accepted model for community corrections. All three models refer to the substitution of formal criminal justice proceedings against an offender with counseling and/or educational programs. The substitution may occur at any level or stage of the criminal justice system (police, courts, corrections). Community-based correctional programs include police discretionary diversion, pretrial diversion, school diversion, restitution, vocational training, probation and parole, and other re-integration programs.

The role of the community in correctional programs depends to a large extent on the interaction between the criminal justice system, political influences, and public attitudes. Community corrections has typically been seen primarily in probation and parole programs. The use of innovative programs such as restitution, community-service programs, and volunteers have increasingly brought the community into a correctional role with offenders.

The development and maintenance of a successful community correctional program relies on a balance between public attitudes, the criminal justice system, and related systems (e.g., education, employment, housing, etc.). While local control is important for community corrections, state-level offices which monitor community control and provide systematic treatment appear to be the most effective approach.

References

Abadinsky, H. (1986). *Probation and parole: Theory and practice,* 3rd ed. Englewood Cliffs, NJ: Prentice-Hall, Inc.

Austin, J. and Krisberg, B. (1981). Wider, stronger and different nets: The dialectics of criminal justice reform. *Journal of Research on Crime and Delinquency,* January:159–60, 170.

Benekos, P. and Merlo, A. (1992). *Corrections: Dilemmas and directions.* Cincinnati: Anderson Publishing Co.

Berry, B. (1985). Electronic jails: A new criminal justice concern. *Justice Quarterly*, 2:1–22.

Bowman, J. and Elliston, F. (1988). *Ethics, government and public policy.* Westport, CT: Greenwood Press.

Bureau of Justice Statistics. (2004). *Probation and parole 1995.* Washington, DC: U.S. Government Printing Office.

Bureau of Justice Statistics. (1990). *Census of local jails, 1988.* Washington, DC: U.S. Government Printing Office.

Burton, V., Dunaway, R. and Kopache, R. (1993). To punish or rehabilitate? A research note assessing the purposes of state correctional departments as defined by state legal codes. *Journal of Crime and Justice* 16(1):177–88.

del Carmen, R. and Vaughn, J. (1986). Legal issues in the use of electronic surveillance in probation. *Federal Probation,* June:60–69.

Carney, L. P. (1977). *Corrections and the Community.* Englewood Cliffs, NJ: Prentice-Hall.

Chaneles, S. (1980). Editorial: On social justice. *Journal of Offender Counseling Services and Rehabilitation*, 4:196.

Fischer, C. (Ed.). (1988). Campaign focus on furloughs prompts review of programs. *Criminal Justice Newsletter*, 9:23.

Galaway, Burt. (1977). The use of restitution. *Crime and Delinquency*, 23(1):57.

Harland, A. T. (1980). Court-ordered community service in criminal law: The continuing tyranny of benevolence? *Buffalo Law Review*, 29(3):425–86.

Hudson, J. and Chesney, S. (1978). Research on restitution: A review and assessment. In B. Galaway and J. Hudson (Eds.), *Offender restitution in theory and action.* Lexington, MA: Lexington Books.

Kappeler, V. and Potter, G. (2005). *Critical issues in police civil liability*, 3rd ed. Long Grove, IL: Waveland Press.

Kinkade, P., Leone, M. and Semond, S. (1995). The consequences of jail crowding. *Crime and Delinquency* 41(1):150–61.

Kratcoski, P. C. et al. (1981). Contemporary perspectives on correctional volunteerism. In P. Kratcoski (Ed.), *Correctional counseling and treatment.* North Scituate, MS: Duxbury Press.

Latessa, E. J. and Allen, H. E. (2003). *Corrections in the community*, 3rd ed. Cincinnati: Anderson Publishing Co.

Lemert, E. M. (1980). Diversion in juvenile justice: What hath been wrought. *Journal of Research on Crime and Delinquency*, January:40.

Logan, C. H. (1990). *Private prisons: Cons and pros.* New York: Oxford University Press.

Martinson, R. (1974). What works?: Questions and answers about prison reform. *Public Interest*, 35:22–54.

McShane, M. and Krause, W. (1995). *Community corrections.* New York: Macmillan.

Newman, D. J. (1978). *Introduction to criminal justice.* New York: Lippincott.

Novack, Steve. (1980). *National assessment of adult restitution programs: Preliminary report 111.* Duluth: University of Minnesota Press.

Petersilia, J. and Turner, S. (1986). *Prisons vs. probation in California: Implications for crime and offender recidivism.* Santa Monica, CA: Rand Corporation.

Petersilia, J., Turner, S., and Kahan, J. (1985). *Granting felons probation: Public risk and alternatives.* Santa Monica, CA: Rand Corporation.

Potter, Joan. (1981). The pitfalls of diversion. *Corrections Magazine*, 7(1):5.

President's Commission on Law Enforcement and Administration of Justice. (1972). *The challenge of crime in a free society.* New York: Avon Press.

Reiff, R. and Reissman, F. (1964). *The indigenous non-professional.* New York: National Institute of Labor Education.

Samaha, J. (1997). *Criminal justice.* St. Paul, MN: West Publishing Co.

Schwartz, M. and Travis, L. (1997). *Corrections: An issues approach.* Cincinnati: Anderson Publishing Co.

Smykla, J. O. (1981). *Community-based corrections: Principles and practices.* New York: Macmillan Publishing Co., Inc.

Smykla, J. and Selke, W. (1995). *Intermediate sanctions: Sentencing in the 1990s.* Cincinnati: Anderson Publishing Co.

Tonry, M. and Hamilton, K. (1995). *Intermediate sanctions in overcrowded times.* Boston: Northeastern University Press.

Whitehead, J. T., Pollock, J. and Braswell, M. (2004). *Exploring corrections.* Cincinnati: LexisNexis/Anderson.

Zupan, L. (1991). *Jails: Reform and the new generation philosophy.* Cincinnati: Anderson Publishing Co.

CASE 1

The Minister and the Ex-Offender

As one of your community's leading ministers, you have always spoken out for progressive correctional reform. Your congregation has usually backed you, and on the few occasions when they did not, they still remained tolerant of your views. Now, however, things are different. Sally, a former member of your church, was once active in working with the church youth. She has since been convicted of embezzlement from the local bank where she worked and sentenced to a year in prison.

As her minister, you kept in contact with her from the beginning of her imprisonment. No one ever really believed she would have to serve time; since the money was returned, no one expected that her boss would even bring charges against her. Everyone has financial burdens at one time or another, and Sally had experienced a succession of problems over a long period of time. The clincher was her husband's permanent disability as a result of an accident. The bills began to pile up faster than she could get them paid. They had mortgaged their house and sold one of their two cars. Finally, in desperation, Sally "borrowed" several thousand dollars from the bank where she had worked as a teller for years. When her crime was discovered, her world crumbled around her.

She has now returned to the community after serving a prison term for embezzlement. When you talked to her the day after she returned, you realized that she was a broken woman. Her daughter had dropped out of school to care for the father, and his disability check was their primary source of income. You counseled her and encouraged her to try to regain her place in the community. You also helped her find work and even suggested that she return to your church, where she had previously been very active. She was reluctant to rejoin the church, fearing rejection by the congregation. You tried to reassure her that everyone was behind her and wanted her to return to the church. In fact, a substantial number of the members had told you as much. When you learned that there would soon be an opening in the Sunday school for a youth director, you asked Sally to consider taking the position. After several days of thinking about it, she agreed.

You have now brought her name before the Sunday school committee and they have, to a person, refused to consider her for the youth leader position. Their bitterness has taken you totally by surprise; their words remain all too clear in your mind: "How would it look to the rest of the community to have an ex-convict directing our youth?" Should you fight for what you believe is right and risk dissension, or should you tell her that her fears are more valid than you had thought; that her former fellow church members have not been able to forgive and forget?

Questions for Discussion

In this particular case you, as the minister, must make a difficult decision. If you insist on Sally being allowed to become a youth leader and the dissenting members relent, what kind of emotional pressure would this put Sally under, and how would she handle it? On the other hand, if you "give in" to the disagreeable committee members and inform Sally of their decision, what impact will your action have on Sally's and your own self-concept, as well as your leadership ability in the church? Perhaps you were not fully aware of the church's true attitude concerning Sally as an ex-offender. How could you have possibly made yourself more aware of their feelings?

Corrections in Jail

You have just received your bachelor of science degree in criminal justice. The curriculum included some courses in corrections as well as the law enforcement core in your emphasis area, so your first job in the jail section of the sheriff's office is not completely alien to you. You feel you have enough basic knowledge to get by, and you are looking forward to the assignment.

The sheriff has three chief deputies: one for criminal activity, one for civil process, and one for the jail. The sheriff requires all new deputies to start in the jail section and work their way into the criminal division where the action is. The jail division has a number of "old-timers"—men who want those "eight to five" duty hours and who are, perhaps, a little too old for the street. But the jailers wear uniforms just like the other deputies, and there is no way to tell the difference when you walk out of the jail section and onto the street. The division also has a retired female licensed practical nurse. All things considered, the day shift in the jail is pretty routine, although there is usually some excitement on weekends.

The jail itself is fairly new, having been financed for the most part by federal and state grant funds. However, it has no recreational facility or any significant community-oriented programs. Therefore, a stay in jail is a stay in custody with very little physical or mental activity. The chief deputy for the jail has initiated his own trustee system in which certain adult prisoners are released to work during the day with little or no supervision. They usually clean up the offices in the jail and the courthouse and wash county cars. Most of the female prisoners work in the kitchen. Those who are new and are not known to the jailers are not released except to walk around the exercise area twice a day.

Your first few weeks pass rapidly and you begin to settle into the routine. However, you are concerned about the waste of human resources caused by not letting more of the prisoners out to work. As you see it, few are dangerous or likely to escape; most are misdemeanants, and many of the offenders are not convicted but are simply awaiting trial because they could not make bail. There are a few who are awaiting grand jury action and could be classified as "pretty tough customers." There are also a few local inmates who are serving out their sentences in the jail.

You decide to approach the chief deputy to see if some sort of voluntary work-release program could be devised to get some prisoners out during the day and have them return at night. You reason that it would save the county money on meals and give the prisoners some sense of self-worth and accomplishment. A prisoner might even be able to make enough to cover the 10% required by the bail bondsman.

The chief deputy for corrections had two pieces of advice when you brought up the subject to him. "Wait till you've been here longer before you bring up ideas like that. And if you don't like it here, go see the sheriff." He was sincere about what he said, too. He had been with the sheriff for seven years, ever since his retirement from the military service. He had carefully formulated his jail regulations to require ease of supervision, the least probability of escape, and the fewest entanglements with lawyers, citizen groups, and the grand jury. Since ease of supervision required restricted movement, the chief deputy's policy was to keep the prisoners in their cells as much as possible and call it "tight security." The other quality his reputation rested on was cleanliness. The jail was spotless and any visitors, including the grand jury, usually commented favorably on its condition and appearance. In fact, most visitors deduced that if the jail was clean, it was well managed; and for the record, one escape in the last two years spoke for itself. The chief deputy was pretty smart all right.

You considered his advice. If the sheriff thinks the idea is good, the chief deputy will undoubtedly accept it. But if it involves a greater risk of having a prisoner walk off, if it involves some degree of community acceptance, and if it involves some planning and legwork with prospective employers, the chief deputy will never really accept it.

You must decide whether or not to draw up a plan and present it to the sheriff, recognizing that his decision would concern more than just the proposal you would be submitting.

Questions for Discussion

In this case, is the prevailing attitude of jail personnel more oriented toward law enforcement or corrections? Does that attitude have anything to do with the sheriff's policy that all new deputies must first be assigned to jail duties? Is there a more subtle way you could have proposed your ideas for improvements, perhaps after you had been employed a while longer?

CASE 3

The Correctional Volunteer

Your job with the department of corrections is interesting and somewhat frustrating. While the community pays a great deal of lip service to the general idea of rehabilitation, there is a strong undercurrent of retributive feelings, especially noticeable in business people who control the community's finances and, therefore, have a great deal of influence upon community attitudes.

You knew that being a volunteer coordinator was going to involve motivating people, but you did not expect such passive ambivalence toward community correctional programs on the part of those who comprise the community power structure. Obviously, you will have to get your program going without much help from the city leaders. You ask yourself, "Where do I start on a problem like this?"

Herbert Smith, now retired, has been a history teacher in the high school for twenty-two years and is well respected by his former students and those in the local business community. Mr. Smith has also taught the adult Sunday school class for fifteen years and has been known to speak out in his low-key way about human rights and other issues involving the importance of human dignity. You are meeting at Mr. Smith's home to discuss the problems you are encountering as a correctional volunteer coordinator.

Mr. Smith is quite supportive of your ideas and, as you had hoped, he agrees to become a member of your volunteer organization.

Although it is hardly necessary, you do a routine records check with the local police and find that Mr. Smith has not even had a parking ticket in the past twenty years. He looks like an ideal volunteer, and if he is successful, there should be many others.

Mr. Smith quickly acclimated himself to the local probation office. Everyone liked him. He was happy to help in any way he could—making coffee, copying records, or running to the courthouse or an errand.

Within six months Herbert was by far the star within a group of a dozen or so volunteers. He ran a parenting group for probationers with small children and even carried a caseload of ten clients under the supervision of Ron, a veteran probation officer.

What you have begun to notice in the last two months are directives from the state director to recruit more volunteers to do tasks formerly done by full-time probation officers. A recent memo represents the "icing on the cake." Your regional supervisor has recommended that Herbert take over two-thirds of Ron's caseload when he retires at the end of the month as a partially compensated volunteer. Reading the memo again, you get an ache in the pit of your stomach. Would Herbert be interested? Should he be? What you had hoped would be an opportunity for the community to get involved in a positive way in the lives of its offenders seems to have evolved into the means of the state for containing costs. You know the state is in something of a financial crunch, but a program that was designed to include members of the community had begun to use them. Was it fair to the volunteers? Was it fair to the regular probation officers? What would be the impact on probationers?

Questions for Discussion

How should you react to your regional supervisor's recommendations? How should your agency balance being cost efficient with cost effectiveness? What impact will such practices have on new college graduates who want to work in the area of community corrections?

The Teacher, the Delinquent and the Gang

Schools have certainly changed since you last taught in the classroom. It used to be short hair, no jeans, no slacks, and no fun! One of the reasons students looked forward to college was that they could do and dress as they pleased. But now, high schools are becoming very similar to college in many respects. Such traditional concepts as study hall and homeroom are beginning to disappear. Many high schools allow students much more flexibility in choosing the courses they take, which is a pleasant change from the school system you recall attending. You remember well how much you hated the conformity. Not only are students now allowed more freedom in choosing courses, but teachers are also allowed more freedom in experimenting with different teaching methods. With a newly earned master of education degree, as a fifty-six-year-old teacher who hasn't taught in more than twenty years, you have a number of ideas on how to improve the quality and interest of classroom instruction. Yet, you realize a twenty-five-year absence is a long time and things have changed since you stopped teaching to raise a family. Your husband, a retired city engineer, cautioned you not to expect too much too soon; nevertheless, you remained optimistic about the possibilities regarding innovating educational techniques.

You found out quickly that some of the changes in contemporary high schools might not have been for the better. When you taught high school, the teacher was considered "boss," and his or her word was usually law. For those few students who did not accept it, there was detention or possible expulsion available to help convince them. Now, however, student discipline seems to be growing weaker, if it exists at all. In fact, your school principal, who believes in strict discipline, has been brought to court twice over being too punitive.

Because the judge in your community also believes in strict discipline, the principal won both cases. However, student behavior has continued to become more aggressive in your high school, as demonstrated by several recent physical assaults on teachers. And to make matters worse, several groups of students have emerged that are beginning to look more and more like gangs.

There appear to be three primary neophyte gangs vying for attention. The first, "The Rosewood Brothers," was apparently inspired by a recent popular film and includes about a dozen young African-American males ranging in age from fourteen to eighteen. The second, the "Border Runners," are comprised primarily of young Latino males whose members seem to be concentrated in the fifteen- to sixteen-year-old range and number about a dozen, also. A third smaller group, the "Invisible Empire," is the name five or six underachieving white male students go by. With their shaven heads, they look like skinhead "wanna-bes." Of course, several girls seem to affiliate with each gang. Other than several fist fights and petty acts of vandalism, there have been no major confrontations. However, recently several members of the "Invisible Empire" have boasted of getting their hands on two AK-47s. Mr. Smith, the principal of your school, seems a little nervous but hopes that several key graduations will take away the leadership of the gangs in question. You aren't so sure.

Against this backdrop, you are currently faced with a significant discipline problem in one of your own classes. A fifteen-year-old female student has consistently refused to cooperate with you regarding course assignments and behavior in the classroom. She hangs around the "Border Runners." At times she is belligerent, and at other times she simply ignores you. And every so often . . . just often enough to give you a faint sense of hope, she contributes something creative and positive to a class discussion. Unfortunately, just as quickly, she reverts to a rebellious act. Needless to say, such behavior encourages other members of the class to be disruptive also. In addition, several members of the "Border Runners" who are also in your class occasionally encourage her to be disruptive.

This particular student has been in trouble with the police since she was ten years old for truancy, occasional shoplifting, and minor vandalism. You have heard that the juvenile court judge has indicated that one more incident will send her to training school for a long stint.

The principal has agreed to have her expelled from school; expulsion would probably result in her being sent to training school.

You are uncertain as to what course of action to take. You would hate to see the student sent to training school, but you doubt other disciplinary measures would do any good. On the other hand, you can accomplish very little in class as long as she continues to misbehave. You have tried to contact her parents, but they do not respond to your personal notes or your phone calls. Her affiliation with the "Border Runners," as well as the larger issue of the emergence of the gangs themselves, concerns you. Something needs to be done, but what?

Questions for Discussion

Are you responsible only as a teacher, or do you also have responsibilities as a concerned citizen? What other social agencies or non-profit organizations might be helpful in this particular situation? Could you possibly work in some way with local law enforcement officials to address the emerging problems concerning some of your students?

A Family of Offenders

Jake is thirteen years old, a little small for his age, yet wise in the ways of the world and as tough as a marine drill sergeant. Jake's usual racket is "protection." For a portion of the other sixth-graders' lunch money, Jake will guarantee that they will not be harassed by the playground bullies, of whom Jake is the most likely hazard.

Since being assigned as a juvenile aftercare worker in the county youth court, you have already seen Jake on several occasions and have heard many stories about his family, which your counterpart in the adult court calls "a breeding ground for felons." If Jake's early conduct is any indication, he will deserve the description of "felon" as soon as the youth court statutes allow.

Jake was not thought to be a proper candidate for a foster home or a group home, so he was committed to the state juvenile training schools on three occasions. His commitment did not seem to have any effect on his subsequent conduct, except that his grades improved after each period.

You decided to visit Jake's home to talk to his mother. It is well known that six of Jake's eight brothers and sisters have served jail sentences, and two brothers are presently in the state penitentiary. Sam, the oldest, is twenty-two years old and is serving eight years for armed robbery. Richard, age nineteen, is serving twenty years for kidnapping and attempted rape of a high school girl who was walking home from school. Jake's two sisters, ages seventeen and eighteen, have long records of shoplifting. The older one was involved in a killing at a local lounge and may be indicted at the next grand jury term.

The specific reason you decided to visit Jake's mother is that he has been associated with a group of four older boys—two of whom are believed to be his brothers—who are thought to be involved in a series of local "lovers' lane" robberies. The robbers always leave the scene on foot. On one occasion, a fourth member of the band, acting as a lookout, ran up to the three who were committing the robbery to warn them of an approaching car. Although identification was incomplete, a composite sketch created a strong implication that Jake was the lookout. The rest of the gang had worn stocking masks.

Jake's family lives in a three-room flat in the ghetto. Mattresses crisscross the floor of the common bedroom, and there is a new color television, "a gift from a friend," his mother said, in the living room and kitchen combination. The third room appeared to be the mother's private bedroom.

The house was dirty, and the furniture in the main room gave the feeling of a waiting room rather than a family-centered area. You gathered that mama was probably in business for herself, and that it was up to the three children who remained at home to take care of themselves. You doubted that your talk with Jake's mother would produce anything except evasiveness and hostility.

Jake's mother, obviously just out of bed for your 1:00 PM appointment, was belligerent and denied any possibility that Jake could be in any trouble, or even heading for trouble. She finally admitted that Jake had been in trouble "once or twice" and then became abusive, blaming the police for her son's trouble. She asked you unceremoniously to "get out and don't come back."

About a month later, Jake and his brothers were arrested by a police undercover team posing as a lovers' lane couple. The juvenile court waived jurisdiction, and Jake was sent to adult court. Although the court-appointed defense attorney attempted to have Jake tried separately, he and his brothers were tried together, and all were sentenced to a term in the state prison for adult males. Because of his youth, Jake's sentence was suspended. You are asked by the adult probation supervisor to help with Jake's supervision (both adult and juvenile probation functions are integrated under the same authority in your state). Although Jake is legally bound to serve an adult's sentence and is responsible to the adult court, you may hold the key to his eventual rehabilitation, or there may be no such key. You want to salvage Jake from a career of crime but the odds do not look good. Is there anything you can possibly do, or should you just write Jake off?

Questions for Discussion

In this case, Jake is quickly becoming just another criminal justice statistic. As a product of a "criminal" environment, Jake seems to be moving toward crime as a career. Could Jake be removed from this environment? Where could he be sent? What would be the consequences of such action on Jake and his family? Are there other alternatives?

The Limits of Responsibility

"Hey, Joe, bring me one of those cigars," you shout, pouring yourself another steaming cup of coffee.

You, Joe, Bob, and Ted had been coming to your lake cottage every Thursday night for the last ten years. Located just thirty minutes from Middleville where you all live, it is a great place to get away. Who says middle-aged men can't have their own clubhouse? Sometimes you drank tea and soft drinks. Other times you and the boys might have a couple of beers. When it was cold, hot coffee tended to be the preferred drink. Whatever the beverage of choice or take-out, your evening together always culminated with the four of you smoking a cigar and talking about whatever came to mind. On a cold February night, you perked, drank, smoked, and talked.

"Fellows, my real estate business has been mighty good to me. My wife and children are healthy and happy. I've got a lot to be thankful for."

"I'll second that thought," Bob echoed. "My hardware store has held its own, and Sue has recovered from her surgery."

Ted, a successful local attorney, reflected on his past year of getting through a difficult case and being able to breathe again. It had also been a pretty good year for Joe, a third-generation cattle farmer.

You continued: "You know, I've been thinking about those homeless folks on the streets this winter. Seems like there are more of them than ever before. And that piece in the paper about the need for a women's shelter. I've been wondering if, with me being so fortunate, maybe I ought to see about helping those folks in some way."

Casually blowing spiraling smoke rings, Bob replied, "God helps those who help themselves."

Joe chimed in, "Don't go getting bleeding-heart liberal on us, John. I'd like to see some of those homeless men out on my farm working like I do. Besides, everyone knows a lot of the homeless are just lazy and as for the women's shelter, they need to take shelter in their own homes and be good mothers and wives."

"I don't know," you reply. "It's awful cold out there. Everyone's not as lucky as we are. I've been thinking about calling Jenny Andrews, the community director of social services, to see if she could use a couple of my empty buildings downtown."

Relighting his cigar, Ted compliments you for your charitable attitude and adds, "Just remember, John, the downtrodden have to want to help themselves. And no matter how many you help, there are always others to take their place. Besides, you need to consider liability issues. No matter how good your intentions are, some people will sue you at the drop of a hat."

"Maybe so, but it seems like we ought to do our part and give something back to our community."

"We do," Bob replied. "We pay taxes and give to charities like the United Way and March of Dimes."

"Come on, John, lighten up," Joe chided.

You smile sheepishly, "OK, but is there something else we could do?"

Questions for Discussion

Do you have a valid point, or should you just let the agencies take care of the problem? Has our society become more or less helpful in dealing with problems like the homeless or victims of abuse? Can you think of any examples?

House Arrest or Probation Revocation?

The court has sentenced Tommy Smith, age twenty-one, for the second time in three years. The first conviction was for unlawful possession of marijuana. When Tommy's mother testified that he was needed to help support the family, the judge suspended the confinement and ordered Tommy to six months' probation. He was ordered to report to you, a state probation officer for the sixth judicial district, as you deemed necessary for his restoration to the community as a productive member. The judge agreed that if the probation was satisfactory and Tommy did not get into any more trouble, he would consider expunging the record, since Tommy was only eighteen years old with no previous convictions.

The probation period went well and the court duly expunged the record, but now Tommy was back in criminal court for the second time. On this occasion he was charged with breaking and entering, a lower degree of burglary in your state. The judge was somewhat exasperated, but considering the fact that this was officially a first offense, he again suspended Tommy's sentence and ordered him to serve four years of supervised probation and make restitution in the amount of value of the items stolen. You felt that the term was somewhat severe, but you know that male offenders in Tommy's age range usually need a great deal of supervision and typically have a higher probability for repetitive criminal behavior than some other groups, and also that burglary is a highly repetitive crime under any circumstance.

Your review of the presentence investigation indicated that Tommy's father disappeared when Tommy was fifteen years old. Soon after the disappearance, Tommy dropped out of high school for a job to help support his mother and his four brothers and sisters. You also noted that Tommy had no juvenile record and still lives at home in a very small but clean apartment in a government-subsidized housing project. Tommy is no longer the only income provider. Two of his younger brothers both have decent-paying jobs and help support the family. One is an assistant manager at a fast-food restaurant and the other is a plumber's apprentice.

Your first interview was with Tommy and his job foreman. Tommy's foreman assured you that Tommy was a good worker and, despite the fact of Tommy's long absence from the job while in jail awaiting trial, he would readily take Tommy back. Tommy also seemed to have a good relationship with his boss and co-workers.

You then visited Tommy's mother in an effort to capitalize on the strong mother-son relationship as an aid in reinforcing a responsible behavioral pattern, especially concerning Tommy's after-hours activities. Tommy's mother seemed to blame her son's criminal activity on a bad crowd in the neighborhood with whom Tommy had recently begun to associate.

As a result of weekly consultations with Tommy and his mother, Tommy appeared to be meeting the conditions of his probation with only minimal difficulty. Unfortunately, because of his apparent love of excitement with his new associates and the easy money to be gained, Tommy was on the court docket again twelve months later; this time for conspiracy and burglary of a railway freight car.

The railway police, noting a huge rise in rail cargo theft, had employed extra security officers to stake out the rail yard under increased but discreet observation in an effort to break up some of the gangs that were looting the boxcars. Tommy was caught on a Saturday night with three friends after breaking into five boxcars. Although nothing was missing from the boxcars, Tommy eventually admitted his intent to steal and implicated his companions in a similar manner. Because of Tommy's cooperation during the investigation, the district attorney decided not to prosecute the case against Tommy.

Now you must decide whether to initiate a revocation hearing. Tommy is a personable young man who just can't seem to say no to the influence of his friends after hours. You could revoke his probation or try another option: house arrest. If you placed him on house arrest during evenings for six months, he might find some new, less trouble-prone friends. Of course, he would have to agree to wear an electronic bracelet for monitoring purposes. You know from experience that house arrest doesn't work for everyone. Some probationers simply ignore or cover the device and go out anyway. However, with the strong support of Tommy's mother and his family, house arrest just might work in his case. In a sense, his probation deserves to be revoked. Yet, what good will it do him or society to serve time in jail or prison? The judge has deferred to your good judgment. The decision is up to you and up to Tommy.

Questions for Discussion

In this case you, as the probation officer, are confronted by the judge's expectations of what your role should be. Apparently, the judge's perceptions are not in complete agreement with yours. Do you and the judge fully understand each other's role as it relates to probation? Could you and the judge better define your professional relationship regarding probationers? What are the limits of technology, such as the use of electronic bracelets, when dealing with probationers?

CASE 8

Community Corrections for Profit?

The sign over the door reads "Professional Corrections Services." Since criminal justice jobs are scarce in your city, you accepted a position as a community probation officer two years ago. The pay wasn't great—about $25,000 a year—nor were the benefits anything to brag about. What sold you in addition to needing a job was the recruiting pitch focusing on making a difference in the lives of offenders and the variety of correctional services you could help to provide. Substance-abuse counseling, DUI school, school prevention programs, and extensive job placement services for offenders who have successfully completed the agency's twelve-month program sounded to you like an energetic, comprehensive environment in which you could gain some work experience.

Your actual experiences over the last two years were a far cry from the personnel director's pitch. Based on your own initiative, you had enjoyed helping some of the offender clients you worked with, but most of your job has been focused on collecting probation fees. Like the agency's probation supervisor, Joe Jackson, once told you with a chuckle, "All you need for this job is a good calculator, a desk lamp, and revocation papers." In fact, the agency's director set up a system that allowed probation officers to double their salaries based on commissions they received as a result of high collection rates from probationers. Such a system encourages probation officers to keep their clients on probation longer than necessary and to enroll them in costly programs that they don't really need. And if that weren't enough, the director's salary is $200,000 a year, not counting his company car and expense account. His hand-picked board of directors—along with their spouses—are treated to a week-long cruise each summer.

Several of the newer probation officers have voiced their frustration to you and plan to report the agency to the state's legislative oversight committee.

Questions for Discussion

You have considered joining the other disgruntled officers in filing a complaint or simply looking for a position with another more professional agency. You need to do something, and sooner rather than later. What might be some advantages to your procuring a position as a state probation officer as opposed to working for a private probation agency? What are some ways the morale of the probation officers in your current agency could be improved?

SECTION III

The Inmate

The next nine cases and text will provide an insight into the world of inmates in prison. All types of persons are present in an inmate population; there are good and bad persons—some who feel a great deal of remorse for their offenses and others who seem to feel no remorse for their crimes. Bullies, drug abusers and embezzlers, as well as former school teachers, lawyers, and doctors comprise the typical prison population. To gain maximum understanding of the inmate in prison, you should attempt to relate to each case as if you were the inmate who is described. The solutions to the problems raised in these cases will become more significant as you put yourself in the inmate's place.

INTRODUCTION

The thoughts of an inmate in a maximum-security prison as described in the following quotation suggest a world in which hope and hopelessness reside in close proximity; a world that is often frustrating for the "keepers" as well as the "kept."

> If prisons are ever to be understood for what they mean and what they do, it will be in terms of human lives. I have been surviving or trying to survive (simple endurance is not survival) a prison term. My consciousness of prison, at the moment, is sunk into the waking routines hammering me in the face day after day. I live in a cell, roughly eight by ten, painted a shade of green. Inside there is a toilet, sink, cabinet, and shelves strewn with pictures of my kids and old, forgotten friends. At night I read 'til tired, if I'm not attending class. After lights out I lay in the dark smoking, listening to the radio, or just thinking of the family.
>
> The worst part of prison life is the pure intensity of waiting. In prison everyone waits for something (mail call, visiting day, his or her release day); the harsh air drains the blood and thoughts sink into nothing. In the evening I stare out at the falling sun, the world fills the window and stops there pressed against my face. My sleeping rhythm is jagged, dreams transmit the fear of all the strangers in my life. The nights in confinement burn my memory down to an essence of fatigue, distorting whatever I recall of my real past. I rummage passionately among faces which come against the night with empty, haunting implosions, homeless like starlight, striking a universe away from sources long melted into the void.
>
> I wake in the hard, white nothingness of morning, mostly taking breakfast, shower, shave, and dress for work. I walk down the steel steps and down the long hallway to my job. I work in the processing and classification area as a test proctor and clerk for the labor department. I do my work such as I have to do within the time span of interruptions, talk, desolate comradeship, and iron-tasting coffee.
>
> Day to day, life for any man locked up can be overwhelming. It is generally boring, lonely, and keenly frustrating as he is deprived of most of his social identity and personal worth. His liberty is restricted to a fenced-in or walled-in compound and even here, he can own very few personal items. His recreation is limited. He must nearly always eat, sleep, and live around and among men he reminds himself repeatedly he would not associate with in free life. Days seem to devour each other, or run by as if under water. The inmate, segregated from a society that he is simultaneously a part of, exists in a kind of regimented tribal commune with its own rules, hierarchies, and inbred morality.
>
> To survive both mentally and emotionally in a prison, one must learn to fear the past more than the future. (Braswell, 1976)

Conflicting correctional philosophies translated into correctional policy (Cullen and Gilbert, 1982), the social/sexual restrictions of prisons (Lockwood, 1983), situations conducive to violence (Fox, 1969; Lockwood, 1980), and problems with the evaluation of strengths and weaknesses of correctional efforts (Glaser, 1971; Johnson, 1987; Shover and Einstadter, 1988)—all contribute to the ambiguity and confusion of the inmate world. A starting point for this world of myriad contradictory realities is the inmate classification process.

INMATE CLASSIFICATION

The essential stigma of being an offender is, of course, a "given" condition that will informally classify most inmates in the eyes of the public as well as the eyes of correctional personnel, from the time of their initial incarceration through their post-release experiences as an ex-offender (Van Voorhis et al, 2004; Whitehead et al., 2004). However, once an inmate is remanded to the custody of a correctional facility, he or she will be formally classified.

An inmate classification process typically includes a number of areas including security concerns, physical health status, a psychological profile, educational level, vocational needs and job-related skills, and one's religious preference. This process requires medical and related health examinations, psychological, educational, and vocational testing, and caseworker reviews. Inmate classification is the single most important function performed by prison staff. While the primary responsibility of any correctional facility is public safety, neither that nor the safety of prison staff and inmates can be effectively accomplished without a highly professional classification process. The following "case summary" provides a general example of the results of an inmate classification procedure:

> **Case Summary:** John Doe—38767
>
> **Current Legal Status:** Convicted 5–8–02 of armed robbery. Serving 10–20 years. One prior conviction (4–26–98) for burglary. Successfully completed. Probated 4–26–04.
>
> **Physical Health:** Medical examination indicates no current problems, although past history of high blood pressure is noted. Dental examination reveals minor gum infection which can be treated effectively at the institutional dental clinic.
>
> **Psychological Profile:** Psychological testing reveals client is currently experiencing mild depression, probably as a result of his recent imprisonment. No suicidal tendencies are indicated. Test

results also suggest the potential for the client to be highly manipulative.

Educational Level: Educational testing indicates client is functioning at a 10th grade level.

Vocational Skills: Client has worked as a construction laborer and carpenter's helper.

Religious Preference: Client is not a member of a denomination, but indicates that he is Protestant.

Recommendation: I recommend a maximum security classification for the first 6 months, reduced to medium after that period of time, contingent on a review of the client's record. The client should also be encouraged to enroll in the G.E.D. preparation program. I also recommend that the client be considered for a work assignment on the new prison gym construction project.

Other areas of concern when classifying inmates include whether or not their crimes were of a violent nature. For instance, some types of sex offenders demonstrate substantial aggressive tendencies and psychological instability. Drug and/or alcohol problems are also often connected to a variety of offender behavior, ranging from "driving under the influence" to child abuse. Alcoholics Anonymous (AA) has provided treatment for inmates with drug and alcohol problems through long-established institutional programs. Differentiating between habitual or career criminals and first-time less serious offenders is another concern of the inmate classification process. Correctional officials usually prefer to keep first-time, less serious offenders separate from more institutionalized inmates whenever possible. Inmate classification is a process that typically begins upon the offender's entry into the prison system and is updated through reevaluation procedures periodically until his or her release.

THE PRISON ENVIRONMENT

Doing time in prison is difficult, particularly for the first-time offender. Once incarcerated in prison, the inmate has two basic choices: (a) become a part of the inmate subculture/society, or (b) attempt to serve one's sentence isolated from the rest of the inmates. Doing time isolated from the inmate population is an option few offenders can tolerate psychologically and emotionally. Becoming a member of the inmate society carries with it certain requirements, including the rejection of the "straight-world" value system of correctional officials (Irwin, 1996). Relationships with correctional personnel are generally supported only in areas that do not threaten inmate solidarity. For example, it may be fine for an inmate to discuss family problems with a counselor, but discussing relationship problems in the cell house might be perceived negatively by other inmates. Much has been written regarding offender and inmate values, including the inclination for such individuals to de-emphasize or even deny responsibility for their behavior, blaming their parents, the victims, society in general, and the prison itself (Fox, 1983; Samenow, 1984; Braswell and Lester, 1987; Sykes, 1994). The inmate value system has two primary goals: (1) getting out as soon as possible, and (2) making life as tolerable as possible while in prison. Getting out could mean anything from parole to escape. Making life tolerable in prison may include affiliating with a particular inmate group, selling illegal goods and providing illegal services, and working with the prison administration in areas of mutual interest and benefit. Inmates serving longer sentences generally receive the best prison work assignments and often try the hardest to maintain effective communication between prison staff and inmates. Potentially explosive areas in prison life where effective communication is particularly important include the quality of prison food, inmate mail services, canteen goods and services, recreational time and activities, and family visitation.

Critical to the quality of life in a given prison environment is the correctional administrative leadership. Administrative leadership in prisons must set policies and regulate activities in two important correctional contexts: (a) security and (b) treatment. Although the current correctional emphasis seems to be more on security and custody than on treatment, rehabilitation and other treatment programs continue to prove indispensable to correctional administrators, both for changing criminal behavior and attitudes and for minimizing inmate adjustment problems in the prison environment (Cullen and Gilbert, 1982). In fact, effective treatment programs can contribute to effective security maintenance by intervening in individual and group inmate crisis situations. Progressive correctional administrators work hard to minimize any conflicts between security officers and treatment professionals which inmates may be able to intentionally or unintentionally exploit. If administrative leaders do not resolve personnel problems effectively, the result is poor morale as well as the potential for staff corruption. Where corruption in a prison environment has been allowed to evolve, correctional personnel have been involved in a variety of illegal and unethical actions ranging from absconding with prison property (e.g., food) to smuggling guns to inmates for escape purposes.

THE EFFECTS OF IMPRISONMENT

The effects of imprisonment are varied. Prisons have often been referred to as "academies" or "training centers" for criminal behavior, since many offenders leave prison possessing more criminal skills than when they entered. For many prison administrators, the real challenge is not to send inmates back to the community better than they were when they arrived in prison, but to simply send them out no worse than when they came in!

Being separated from family relationships and from heterosexual options often creates major emotional distress. Fear or actual victimization, including sexual or other physical assault from inmates, contributes additional mental and emotional trauma for a number of offenders. Racial tension, substandard living quarters, and inadequate treatment programs also create a negative climate sometimes referred to as the "pains of imprisonment" (Johnson and Toch, 1988).

Prison life is fundamentally different from life on the "outside." Prisons are total institutions where every aspect of basic social activities such as sleeping, working and leisure activities are all performed at the same time in the same place with the same people (Goffman, 1961; Quinn, 2003; Whitehead et al., 2004).

A significant effect of imprisonment concerns the development of informal inmate organizations and associations. These associations develop and evolve for three primary reasons: (1) the offenders are alienated and isolated from society; (2) the prison environment creates common problems of adjustment which require mutual support and cooperation for their solution; and (3) inmates, as members of a formal system, cannot initiate and coordinate their behavior through the formal organization because of who they are (inmates) and where they are (prison) (Samaha, 1997; Braswell et al., 2005). Informal social control results from the development and evolution of informal inmate organizations. The potency of this process of social control depends to a large extent on inmate relations with the security and treatment personnel in a given prison. While existent to some extent in any prison environment, informal inmate social control seems to be less centralized in institutions that have substantial treatment programming and security supervision.

Inmates who have served extended periods of time in prison often become "institutionalized." It does not seem hard to understand that if an offender spends 10 of his or her last 15 years in a prison, then prison isa where his or her friends will be. In addition, because of the highly regimented nature of prison life, institutionalized offenders may experience a phobic reaction to outside or "free-world" life. Such regimentation, while perhaps often necessary, appears to encourage obedience in inmates rather than discipline. Obedience is defined here as responding to external cues (e.g., "following orders") as opposed to discipline, which involves an internal value system allowing the offender to take more responsibility for his or her actions. After years of being told when to do such things as eat, sleep, go to work, and visit with one's family, it is not surprising that inmates find it difficult to take responsibility for such decisions when released into outside society.

Imprisonment appears to encourage a number of role patterns which can be identified among inmates. These patterns or coping roles help offenders to organize their lives in a meaningful way during confinement. Coping roles fall into three basic categories: (1) outsiders, (2) insiders, and (3) changers.

The "outsiders" cope with prison life by viewing confinement as a temporary loss of freedom. Confinement is a pause in their outside lives, to which they plan to return. They accept their confinement, serve their time, are released, and return to their home and original lifestyle. The outside group of offenders probably includes over half of the inmate population. They avoid trouble with other inmates and the correctional staff by doing just what they have to do to realize their goals. They "mind their own business" when it involves other offenders and generally refuse to become involved in other inmates' problems. Outsiders are inclined to obey both formal rules and regulations of the institution and the informal "codes" of inmate society. Outsiders have few inmate friends and refuse to allow the correctional staff to become "intimate" with them. Outsiders want to gain their freedom as quickly as possible and will do nearly anything to increase the chances of early release. One "game" outsiders play for an early release is referred to as "conning the counselors." Inmates learn to say what correctional officers, staff, and counselors want to hear. In this way, the correctional staff believes the inmate has progressed in rehabilitative efforts and are supportive of the inmate's bid for parole.

The "insiders" cope with prison life by viewing confinement as the real world. The outside life has nothing to offer the "insider" inmate. Insiders tend to cope better in confinement than in the outside world. The insiders are considered "losers" on the outside. The insiders develop their own social environment within the walls of prison. Inside, they are somebody. They hold power, wealth, and influence among other inmates.

The third role pattern is the "changers." The changers view confinement as an opportunity to better themselves, to change. They want to learn how to adapt better to the outside and to make a new life for themselves. They participate voluntarily and enthusiastically in programs available to them during confinement. They are attracted to the change programs offered at the correctional institution dealing with therapy, vocational training and education. The changers number less than one-fourth of the inmate population and are generally older than the other inmates (Jarvis, 1978).

INMATE VIOLENCE

In the twenty-first century, new demographic profiles have emerged for inmates. The public demand for stiffer penalties for violent crimes and drug offenses have greatly impacted the prison environment. More violent prisoners are in prison, and prisons are continually being overcrowded. More violent prisoners have resulted in more inmate violence, more violence toward inmates by correctional officers, and more correctional officers being assaulted by inmates (Lawrence, 1991). In addition, the high number of gang members convicted of violent crimes and drug offenses has brought more street gang members into prison, making gangs in prison stronger and more cohesive.

One response to the increased violence in prisons has been the rapid proliferation of so-called "supermax" institutions. These facilities are used to house the most dangerous, disruptive offenders, under the most stringent and austere circumstances. Confined to small, cramped cells for twenty-three hours a day, exercised in restraint gear in dog-run-like exercise pens, severely restricted from enjoying family visitations and other privileges—all are hallmarks of life in supermax. Yet critics of this approach worry that all supermax does is take behavior problems and make them worse.

Racial hatred in prison continues to be a concern for prison administrators. Early prison research did not mention problems with race relations. However, the situation has worsened. There are far more African-American inmates than all other races combined. African-American prisoners may tend to be more assertive and more organized than their white and Hispanic counterparts. Most violence among inmates occurs between different races, with African-Americans the aggressors (80% of recorded incidents) against whites (Lockwood, 1980; Samaha, 1997). White prisoners tend to be less organized, less likely to know other whites in prison, and less willing to band together for protection, making them easier targets for violent confrontations.

SUMMARY

The prison inmate's world is often confusing and ambiguous. The prison environment is often frustrating for the correctional staff as well as for the inmate population. Most offenders are classified informally by the public and correctional personnel as "convicts." Such a label may remain with the offender far longer than the sentence he or she received. A new prison inmate is formally classified during the first few weeks of prison. This classification scheme typically includes a number of areas including security concerns, physical and mental health profiles, educational background, vocational skills, religious affiliations, and type of offense(s) committed. Such classification procedures are performed so that the correctional staff can recommend treatment programs.

The prison environment is difficult for inmates, particularly first-time offenders. The prison culture is unique among all subcultures. In order for inmates to live and cope within the walls, they must make one of two basic choices: (a) become a part of the inmate subculture, or (b) attempt to serve their sentence isolated from the rest of the other inmates. An inmate with a lengthy sentence may find isolation an intolerable experience. Therefore, most inmates find it necessary to adjust and gain membership within the inmate society. The inmate value system has two primary goals: (1) getting out of prison as soon as possible, and (2) making life as tolerable as possible while in prison. Inmates learn quickly how to act with other inmates and how to act with correctional staff. An inmate's relationship with other inmates and the correctional staff is usually based on these two primary goals.

One of the more significant effects of imprisonment concerns the development of informal inmate associations. These associations develop and evolve for three primary reasons: (1) the offenders are alienated and isolated from society; (2) the prison environment creates common problems of adjustment requiring mutual support and cooperation for their solution; and (3) inmates, as members of a formal system (prison), cannot initiate and coordinate their behavior because they are inmates. Inmates who have served extended periods of time in prison often become "institutionalized." Such inmates find greater satisfaction and reward by being in prison than on the "outside."

Imprisonment seems to encourage three basic coping roles for inmates: (1) outsiders; (2) insiders; and (3) changers. The outsiders view prison life as a temporary setback in their lives and plan to return to the outside society. The outsiders comprise the majority of inmates. Insiders view prison life as the "real world." Insiders tend to cope better in the prison than in society. The changers view prison as an opportunity to change their lives for the better and adapt back into society as a rehabilitated person. The changers number less than one-fourth of the inmate population and are generally older than the other inmates.

References

Braswell, M. (1976). *Thoughts from prison.* Hattiesburg, MS: Fox Publishing Co.

Braswell, M. and Lester, D. (1987). *Correctional counseling.* Cincinnati: Anderson Publishing Co.

Braswell, M. J., Pollock, J. and Braswell, S. (2005). *Morality stories.* Durham, NC: Carolina Academic Press.

Cullen, F. and Gilbert, K. (1982). *Reaffirming rehabilitation.* Cincinnati: Anderson Publishing Co.

Fox, V. (1983). *Correctional institutions.* Englewood Cliffs, NJ: Prentice-Hall, Inc., p. 136.

———. (1971). Why prisoners riot. *Federal Probation*, 35:9–14.

Glaser, D. (1971). Five practical research suggestions for correctional administrators. *Crime and Delinquency*, January:32–40.

Goffman, E. (1961). *Asylums: Essays on the social situation of mental patients and other inmates.* Garden City, CA: Anchor Books.

Irwin, J. (1996). The prison experience: The convict world. In G. Bridges, J. Weis, and R. Crutchfield, eds. *Criminal justice.* Thousand Oaks, CA: Pine Forge Press.

Jarvis, D. (1978). *Institutional treatment of offenders.* New York: McGraw-Hill Book Co.

Johnson, R. (1987). *Hard time: Understanding and reforming the prison.* Monterey, CA: Brooks/Cole.

Johnson, R. and Toch, H. (1988). *The pains of imprisonment.* Prospect Heights, IL: Waveland Press, Inc.

Lawrence, R. (1991). The impact of sentencing guidelines on corrections. *Criminal Justice Policy Review* 5:220.

Lockwood, D. (1980). *Prison sexual violence.* New York: Elsevier.

Samenow, S. (1984). *Who he is and how he thinks.* Audiotape. Fayetteville, NC: Psychological Associates.

Samaha, J. (1997). *Criminal justice.* St. Paul, MN: West Publishing Co.

Shover, N. and Einstadter, W. (1988). *Analyzing American corrections.* Belmont, CA: Wadsworth Publishing Co.

Sykes, G. (1994). The society of captives: A study of a maximum security prison. In T. Clear and G. Cole, eds. *American corrections.* Belmont, CA: Wadsworth Publishing Co.

Van Voorhis, P., Braswell, M. and Lester, O. (2004). *Correctional counseling and rehabilitation*, 5th ed. Cincinnati: LexisNexis/Anderson.

Whitehead, J. T., Pollock, J. and Braswell, M. (2004). *Exploring corrections.* Cincinnati: LexisNexis/Anderson.

Bust or Parole?

Your name is Nancy. You are forty-five years old and have served twelve years of a twenty-year sentence for armed robbery. This is the second time around for you. The last time you were in the "joint" was for burglary; you did three years on that sentence and made parole. You stayed straight for almost two years before you got into trouble again. Several of your friends finally convinced you to go along as the lookout on an easy bank score. Unfortunately, it did not turn out to be so easy. The bank's security officers opened fire on your two friends as they left the bank, killing one of them and wounding the other. You quickly surrendered without a struggle. You knew armed robbery was not for you, and you have always regretted your involvement in that particular event. In fact, you have been regretting it for twelve years.

The twelve years you have served on your present sentence have not been easy ones. The inmates in the prison you are in are a new breed, generally younger and more aggressive. Violence on the inside has increased; there are more suicides and assaults than ever before. Although the years have been hard, you have tried to make the most of them. You have earned your high school diploma and have even taken several additional college-level courses in accounting, but in response to the public's demand to "get tough" on crime, many education and recreation programs have been severely cut back or discontinued altogether. This has made the general environment inside worse than ever.

Your brother, who owns a small business, has offered to employ you if you make parole. With your good behavior, your personal efforts toward rehabilitation, and your brother's offer, your chances of making parole are excellent. You realize that you have to stay straight this time or resign yourself to spending most of your remaining years in prison. You really want to make it this time, but there is some trouble brewing in your cell house that could blow your chances for parole sky high and even pose a threat to your own life.

A great deal of illegal drug activity is going on in your cell block. Although drug traffic in most prisons is rather common, in your institution the correctional officers are heavily involved in the illicit drug sales and distribution. An increasing number of women are also submitting to sex with several of the male officers as a means of paying for the drugs and, in some cases, earning extra money. In fact, rumor has it that the chief of security is behind most of it, and that many of the lieutenants and captains turn their heads. The word is also out that many regular and undercover state narcotics agents are presently conducting an investigation. In fact, one new female resident is rumored to be working for the state drug task force. The problem is compounded for you since your cell block is the site of the majority of drug activity.

You have considered going to the prison superintendent, Dr. Smith, who you are certain is not involved in the drug traffic. You know him to be an experienced and progressive corrections administrator. You are really beginning to get uptight because the prison grapevine says that a bust is imminent. Since your cell mate and other inmates in your cell block are heavily involved in drugs, you could be implicated by association. You can sit tight or go to Dr. Smith and tell him what is going on. You wonder whether or not you can really trust the superintendent. If you do tell him what is going on, will he believe you? Will he return you to the cell block to be at the mercy of those inmates and correctional officers you reported? A bust might well ruin your chances for parole. A trip to Dr. Smith might help your chances for parole or, on the other hand, endanger your personal safety.

Questions for Discussion

Nancy is in a dilemma not primarily of her making. Are there outside persons Nancy could go to? Who is really responsible for the correctional officers' involvement? How do you think this kind of corrupt situation develops in prison, and what can be done to provide safeguards against such corrupt practices?

Six Months to Go

Six months ago the biggest concern in your life was finishing college. Now your biggest concern is you own personal safety. Never in a million years did you dream that you would be spending the twentieth year of your life in a state prison. As sociology major in college you studied about crime, criminals, and prisons, but that was nothing compared to your situation now. The constant noise of steel and concrete; the smell of bodies, cigarettes, and old buildings; the inability to go where you want to go, eat what you want to eat—all this is foreign and confusing to you.

Sure, you smoked some grass and sometimes used pills to stay up and study for exams when you were in college; a lot of other students did the same. You never expected to get "busted" for selling a small amount of marijuana and uppers to an acquaintance who turned out to be a narcotics officer. But you did. Since it was your first offense, your lawyer said probation was a sure thing. Unfortunately for you, however, you got a judge who was fed up with drug abuse. He decided that it was time to crack down, and he used you for an example. As a result, he sentenced you to three years in the state prison. When he pronounced sentence, the sky fell for you and your family.

Your experiences in prison have left you confused and frustrated. During those first few months of incarceration, you felt hopeless and alone. Your family, although upset and embarrassed, has stuck by you. It was the efforts of a young prison counselor and the support of your family that have kept you going. Only six months remain on your sentence before you come up for parole. You have "kept your nose clean" with the prison staff and other inmates.

Last night a terrible incident occurred: your eighteen-year-old cell mate, Sam, was brutally raped and beaten by four older inmates, who informed you that the same fate would be yours if you reported them. You remember only too well the whistles and the threats directed toward you during the first several days you were in the cell block. You realize that your size and former athletic conditioning allowed you to establish a relative amount of independence in the prison; your cell mate, being smaller and weaker, had no such natural defense qualities. You also realize that if you report what they did to your friend, the four inmates are likely to make good their threat. Still, you cannot rid yourself of the rage and sickness you feel because of your friend's humiliation and helplessness. You know that he might be attacked again. Yet, you are also confronted with your own needs of survival and well-being.

The only employee you trust in the prison is the young counselor. Not having been at the prison very long, he has only limited influence with the prison administration. Nevertheless, he is enthusiastic and well intentioned. You cannot forget what happened to your cell mate, yet with only six months before parole, you are also thinking of your own welfare.

You have continued to be an avid reader while incarcerated. While in the prison law library doing some research for a fellow inmate, you came across some interesting information concerning a federal law called the Prison Rape Elimination Act. Perhaps this law is intended to assist inmates who are sexual assault victims, like your cell mate.

Questions for Discussion

What does the Prison Rape Elimination Act require of prison officials in protecting inmates from the threat of sexual assault? Did the administration do enough to protect Sam from such abuse? What programs or other opportunities could have been provided for most of the prison's inmates that might have helped alleviate the problem of sexual assault?

CASE 3

An Expression of Grief

You are known as Willy throughout the prison, and you are serving ten to fifteen years on a manslaughter conviction. Before your present conviction, you were sentenced to probation on an assault and battery charge. Now a model inmate, you stick pretty much to yourself and give no one any trouble. Since being in prison you have become interested in religion and spend a great deal of your time reading and studying the Bible.

You recently began receiving weekly letters from your younger sister concerning your father, who was hospitalized again for a terminal liver ailment. Rereading the letters brought back many memories of your childhood. Your father worked long and hard in the coal mines of Kentucky to support his wife and seven children. Although you know you have been pretty much of a failure with your life, you still have a tremendous amount of respect for your father. You decided to request a special pass from the warden to visit your sick and dying father.

The warden considered your request but felt that your maximum security classification, and his own difficulties in having to run a prison that was understaffed, necessitated his rejecting it. Needless to say, you were quite upset. You felt frustrated and helpless.

Several days later the sky fell in. You received a call from your sister telling you that your father had died and that the funeral would be in two days. You again approached the warden, to get permission to attend your father's funeral. The warden sympathized with your plight but again declined your request, for the same reasons given previously. You flew into a frustrated rage, and the guards had to subdue you while the prison physician gave you a sedative. The assistant warden in charge of treatment then had a guard escort you to the chapel for personal counseling with the institutional chaplain, Reverend Jones.

You are now waiting for the chaplain. Visibly upset, you remain silent as you sit there by yourself. You know from other inmates that security is weak in this area of the prison. Should you sneak out the back entrance of the chapel and hide in the milk truck that is parked there each morning? Every inmate in the institution knows about this escape route, and you now have the opportunity to take advantage of it. What should you do? Sure, they would pick you up in a couple of days, but not before you got home for your father's funeral. Of course, you wouldn't make trustee in six months as the warden has promised. Your positive prison record wouldn't be so positive anymore. But what is more important, your father's funeral or your prison record? You sit there, hurt and confused, trying to decide what your next move will be.

Questions for Discussion

What could the administration have done differently to ease the crisis situation with Willy? Could they have let him talk with his father on the telephone? Should he have been left alone in the chapel? Should they have provided counseling services for him at an earlier date?

Something for Nothing

Your name is Billy Denver. Your mother, a registered nurse, divorced your father years ago. Although she had several relationships with other men in the years following the divorce, none ever worked out on a permanent basis. She also had several bouts with alcohol and amphetamine abuse. As if that was not enough, you have not seen your father since the divorce.

You have always had an easy smile. Everyone has always remarked how easygoing you are, how well you roll with the punches. Sure, you have gotten in trouble several times. Once you and two friends were caught joyriding in a car that was not yours, and twice you were apprehended for possession of a substantial quantity of amphetamines. The judge described your third possession charge as the last straw as he sentenced you to nine months in the city jail. You smiled politely as you received your sentence, thinking that the city jail could not be any worse than the boring high school you have been attending.

When you arrived for processing at the jail you were surprised and confused at the whistles and catcalls the other inmates gave you as you walked with the guard through the recreation yard to your cell block.

Eighteen years old, with long straight hair and a fair complexion, you just smiled back and gave the peace symbol in hopes of letting the other prisoners know that you wanted to get along with them.

The next morning the control-station guard sounded the bell and opened the gates as the inmates poured out of their cells, heading for the chow hall. Since you were not hungry, you decided to stay in your cell and read a western you had borrowed from one of your cell mates.

You look up from your book to find a big burly inmate standing in your doorway. "Hi kid," he says with a cold stare.

"Hello. My name is Billy Denver," you respond, eager to make your first friend.

"I know," the visitor replies. "My name is Tom. Most guys in here call me 'Big Tom.'" He goes on to explain to you that things are different in jails and prisons, in ways that people on the outside cannot understand. He continues to stress that in order to have a "safe stay," it is best to have good friends that will stand up for you.

Although you do not completely understand what Big Tom is trying to say, you are relieved at having made a friend so quickly. Tom notices the book in your hand and inquires if you like to read. You indicate that you do and that you hope to read your way through your sentence if you can get enough books. Big Tom assures you that you will not have any problem getting books, since he is personal friends with the jail's librarian. As he describes the kinds of books he likes to read, Tom reaches into his shirt pocket and pulls out a pack of cigarettes. Lighting one, he asks you if you smoke. "Only menthol," you reply. Tom assures you that he can supply you with plenty of menthol cigarettes, since the guy who works in the inmate canteen owes him a number of favors.

As Tom turns to leave, he says, "It gets very lonely in here, Billy, and we have to take care of each other. Just remember, Big Tom takes care of his own. You just be my friend." Needless to say, you are a little overwhelmed by his concern and generosity concerning some of the things he said to you. Should you respond to his friendship? What will he want in return? He does seem to know the ropes. What will happen if you decide to remain somewhat aloof and do your time by yourself?

Questions for Discussion

Is doing time primarily a matter of survival, in which an inmate must learn how to "get along?" Are there limits to what you, as Billy, should be willing to do, and if so, how do you impose those limits?

CASE 5

Showdown at Seven o'Clock

You have been in the state prison for six years. Most of the black inmates in your prison recognize you as their leader, a status which has been yours since one night when the former leader tried to set you up in the showers. It was an unfortunate incident, especially for him. Having been tipped off, you and several of your friends got the best of him and his henchmen. You were injured in the fracas, and he was killed. The results of the whole mess were that you received two additional years for voluntary manslaughter and that you emerged as the primary black leader for the inmates in your prison. The additional time did not mean that much to you, since you were already pulling two concurrent life sentences for a previous shoot-out on the streets where two bank guards were killed. For many reasons you did not really want the leadership role, but there were some advantages to it. Besides having the respect of the other inmates, life in general was a little easier. Being on top brought special favors from the other inmates and special consideration from the correctional staff as well.

In the two years you have been the leader, you have had to deal with a number of problems and issues, including militant young blacks, the Black Muslims, and rival groups. The white inmate group called "The Brotherhood" has created the most problems for you. There have been several confrontations with them, complete with bloodshed and death. In spite of these conflicts and a rigid and disinterested warden, for the most part the lid has been kept on the powderkeg of the prison. In a strange way, you are proud of your efforts toward keeping some measure of peace among the various inmate factions. You are especially proud of how you and the white inmate leader helped the administration avert a major racial confrontation when the prison cell blocks were forced to desegregate by federal court order. You even received a special letter of commendation

84

from the State Corrections Commissioner. But all that was yesterday. Now another confrontation is building up.

Young militants in your group and in the white group are planning an all-out war over the use of the prison band instruments. Your group's "soul" band and the white group's "country and western" band have always had something of a running feud, but now the situation has gotten out of hand and is about to explode. You and the white inmates' leader, Ray, would like to avoid the bloodshed of an all-out riot. However, both of you are having trouble controlling the younger inmates in your respective groups, and the prison administration is not providing much help. In fact, word has come down from the warden that it is up to you and Ray to control your people. The showdown is to take place at seven o'clock in the dining hall. You want to avoid bloodshed, but you also have to maintain the confidence of the black inmates you represent. Tonight in the dining hall all hell may break loose! You cannot back down, and compromise is becoming more difficult as seven o'clock draws nearer. The minutes are ticking away.

Questions for Discussion

How does this situation reflect the changes that have taken place in prisons today regarding violence between inmates? Is there anything the administration could do that might help the black and white leaders maintain peace?

CASE 6

What's for Supper?

Your name is Harriet, but most of the other girls at the state women's prison call you Sis, an affectionate nickname you have earned because you have been a "big sister" to most of the girls in the prison, especially the younger ones. You come up for parole in two months, and you have been told that your chances are good. You have completed three years of a five-year sentence for voluntary manslaughter. One of the many drunken squabbles between you and your husband had ended with you holding a gun in your hand and him lying dead on the floor. Although the nightmares still come from time to time, you can live with what happened now. It is behind you. Besides, you have a nine-year-old daughter who is living with your mother and waiting patiently for your return. Helping the other girls at the prison has been therapeutic for you. You are proud of their confidence in you and your established reputation of being firm but offering an understanding ear.

The food at your institution has never been good, but now it is becoming unbearable. The meals consist mostly of starches; meat is served infrequently and is always of inferior quality. The poor selection of food is bad enough, but the preparation is even worse. Since you are a respected leader of the other inmates, it had fallen to you to go to the prison superintendent and complain.

Rather than offering assurances that she would look into the complaints, she told you to file a grievance and snapped that since she had not received any grievances in writing, you must simply be trying to stir up trouble. As she turned to walk away, the superintendent asked if you didn't have a parole coming up soon.

Tensions continued to mount. For many of the girls, mealtime was the high point of their day. The repeated disappointment of receiving stale bread, gristle, and not enough coffee created a potentially explosive situation. Each mealtime in the dining room was becoming more tense. There had already been several minor confrontations between the inmates and the guards.

Now a group of girls have asked you to endorse a dining-hall protest over the poor food. Because of the high level of emotions, you realize that the protest could easily escalate into a full-blown disturbance. You are sitting on a powder keg that could explode during any meal. You know there is reason to protest, but you also realize that if a serious disturbance occurs, you and the others might lose more than you can ever hope to gain, including your parole. On the other hand, the superintendent and her administration have failed to make any significant improvements regarding the food quality.

If you do not support the protest, you might lose the respect of the girls. Should you approach the superintendent again? Should you just sit tight and see what happens? Should you go ahead and endorse the protest, hoping that it remains peaceful? There is no easy way to go, and time is running out.

Questions for Discussion

Many riots have started in prison mess halls. Could the superintendent have done more to address the complaints about the food? Should you have relied so much on the inmate grievance system? Is it too late to avert the prospect of a mess-hall confrontation?

CASE 7

Home Sweet Home

Next Wednesday you will be walking out those front gates as a free man. This last time around cost you ten years. It was your third hitch. You have spent thirty of the last forty years of your life behind bars. Sixty-two years of life's ups and downs have softened your disposition. You have no excuses left; you feel that the time you got was coming to you. In fact, the last hitch was one you purposely set up.

When you were released the last time, it was a cold gray morning in February. There was no one on the outside waiting for you; your friends were all in prison. You had been divorced for over fifteen years and your former wife had remarried. Your parents were dead, and your two sisters had given up on you long ago. Besides, there were too many decisions to make in the free world. You were not used to all of that freedom; it was frightening. No one cared about you like they did inside the joint.

You got a job as a busboy in a restaurant, but the hustle and bustle was too much, and besides, no one wanted to make friends with an old ex-con. Finally you had all you could take, so you stole all the money from the cash register one night during a lull in the business. You did not spend any of it, but instead you went home, had a beer, and waited. In less than two hours, the police arrived at your apartment. Once the restaurant manager realized you and the money were missing, it was not long before you were arrested. You refused an attorney and told the judge that you would keep committing crimes until he sent you back. He reluctantly sentenced you to ten years. You passed up parole each time it came around.

So here you are again. You have been measured for your new suit of street clothes and your $150 check for transitional expenses has been processed. The labor department representative has arranged for you to have a stock-clerk job in a small grocery store in a nearby town. Your social worker has also arranged for you to stay in a small apartment near where you will work. You remember your last prerelease counseling session with her and how she offered all the words of encouragement a young, energetic, and well-meaning counselor could muster. You just smiled and nodded your approval. What good would it have done to burst her idealistic bubble? She could never understand how frightening the outside world had come to be for you. All of her friends lived in the free world; none of yours did.

You would like to make it on the outside if you could, but the odds are against you. And besides, it's just too lonely out there. You know you ought to feel happy about leaving prison, but the truth is, you are miserable about it. You would like to be able to make it on the outside, but deep down inside you feel you are doomed before you start.

Questions for Discussion

What prerelease programs are available in the prison that would assist this inmate in preparing for release to the outside world? Are there any "life skills" programs available through the prison education and/or treatment services departments? Is there a community-based intensive supervision program (ISP) that he can be referred to by his parole officer once he returns home? Would a halfway house placement be a suitable initial placement for him upon release from prison?

The Prison Schoolhouse

You have been the director of education programs at Anyville State Prison for quite a number of years. The basic education and vocational classes follow a standard public-school schedule. Recruiting qualified teachers is not always easy, given the environment they are asked to work in. Each year you send the annual school calendar to the warden for his information. There has never been a problem in the past with this, but this year is different. A new warden recently took over, coming in with a reputation of being very autocratic and demanding. He calls you to his office one morning to discuss the school schedule.

Without affording you an opportunity to address the issue, the warden tells you to change the schedule. He is irate that the school will be closed from the 18th of December until January 3 for the holidays. He pointedly makes it clear that the prison is not a public school, that it operates "24/7," and he can't afford to have inmates sitting around doing nothing for three weeks. When you try to explain that the inmates and staff both need the break, he refuses to budge. Then you warn him that it is difficult to recruit and retain good teachers, and that something like this could cause some of them to leave. He tells you they can all quit if they don't like it. As you get up to leave his office, the warden tells you ominously that he had better see inmates and teachers in school throughout the holidays.

Questions for Discussion

In addition to a less-than-understanding management style, it is obvious that the warden does not grasp the necessity of a break in the education routine during the holidays. What should (or can) you do?

From Troublemaker
to Peacemaker

As deputy warden of State Prison, it is your responsibility to make a recommendation to the warden regarding Raymond Angelo's request to be allowed to return to the general-population section of death row.

Angelo's correctional history is quite a story. For the last seven years, he has been for the most part isolated in administrative segregation on death row. He was originally sentenced to 10 years for drug dealing and armed robbery, but that was before he was implicated in the killing of a correctional officer.

For the first three years of his prison sentence, Raymond Angelo was a rabble rouser and troublemaker and on the wrong side of just about every correctional officer he came in contact with. Then Officer Edward Klein was stabbed to death. The inmate who stabbed him indicated to investigators that Angelo provided the shank used to kill Officer Klein.

When all was said and done, the inmate who stabbed the correctional officer was sentenced to life without parole and Raymond Angelo was sentenced to death. Sometimes, you think to yourself, justice moves in strange and unpredictable ways.

Angelo raised so much hell during his first six months on death row that he was placed in the administrative segregation unit. That was before he got religion. Over the next two years, Angelo changed—meditating, praying, and reading religious literature instead of shouting and demanding. Then Angelo wrote a best-selling book on spiritual transformation and donated all the profits to a fund set up for Officer Klein's family. To top things off, it looks like his appeals may just carry some weight with the current court.

It seems simple enough—six years of good behavior should get Angelo transferred back into death row's general population, where he could have more privileges. The problem is that correctional offic- ers have long memories when one of their own is killed, and rightly so. While some of the officers who have worked around Angelo are all right with his transfer, most of the other officers are against any change of status for him.

Questions for Discussion

No question about it—you depend more on your correctional officers than on inmates, and you can't deny you have a warden's natural sense of suspicion about Angelo. Still, you want to do the right thing, and it isn't like you would be giving Angelo a walk. What will your decision be?

The Correctional Officer

The correctional officer is an important key to the success of any correctional program. Correctional officers are not only responsible for institutional and program security, they also have tremendous potential as "change agents" of the behavior and attitudes of the inmates they supervise.

In the next eight cases and text you will learn of some of the demands placed on the typical correctional officer. Crisis intervention skills, peer group pressures, and riot control are examples of the situations presented to elicit your reaction.

INTRODUCTION

The impact correctional personnel, particularly security officers, have on the rehabilitation and resocialization of offenders is too frequently given only brief recognition by authorities in the correctional treatment process. In correctional institutions, correctional security personnel have the most contact and interaction with offenders and, therefore, the greatest impact upon them (Jacobs and Crotty, 1983). Although correctional officers frequently are more appreciated by offenders, at the same time they also seem to illicit more resentment (Hawkins, 1976; Ross, 1981; Williamson, 1990). It is not surprising to find former prisoners who could not remember their prison counselor's or caseworker's names but could recall vividly the names and personalities of many of the correctional officers. Despite the well-recognized importance of correctional officers in the correctional process, little is known about their influence on correctional goals.

CORRECTIONAL OFFICERS

Over two-thirds of the employees in corrections are employed in correctional institutions as correctional officers. In terms of sheer numbers, as well as their significant impact on offenders, security personnel are an extremely important component of the correctional workforce. In fact, the correctional officer is the single most powerful, influential force in the prison. The mood of the inmate population, the general environment—all are shaped and influenced by the correctional officer.

While the number of correctional officers increased at a fraction of the rate of increases for inmates over the last twenty years, records are being set in employment. The correctional officer ranks in the upper twenty occupations in terms of growth. It was correctly predicted that a shortage of qualified and motivated personnel in corrections during the 1990s would result in a need to offer increased compensation and benefits, and to make the work of correctional officers more satisfying and rewarding. While predictions on shortages were correct, correctional systems in the United States have yet to achieve increased compensation and benefits for qualified correctional officers (Bureau of Labor Statistics, 2005).

The fact that fewer correctional officers are from minority racial groups appears to be the result of complex social causes. Since many correctional institutions are located in more remote rural areas and draw their employees from the surrounding area, fewer minorities are often employed. A common complaint among convicts is that rural guards from the small towns where prisons are located do not understand the inmate who generally comes from the city (May, 1976; Weisheit, Falcone, and Wells, 2006).

Some people believe that the job of "prison guard" attracts persons who have emotional or personality defects, an image probably produced more by Hollywood than by actual experiences. An earlier study of guards in a maximum-security prison reported that "there is no indication that one type of individual, in terms of personality makeup, is attracted to seek employment in the penitentiary . . ." (Motivans, 1963).

Although this situation may be currently changing for the better, in the past, few individuals aspired to become correctional officers and many did so only under pressure of unemployment or job security (May, 1976). In most prisons, the bulk of the population is poor and economically disadvantaged. In this respect, the prisoners are probably similar to their keepers, since correctional officers are also employed primarily from economically disadvantaged regions. Correctional officers working in federal prisons fare better than their state-employed counterparts (May, 1976). Entry requirements for correctional officer positions may vary from state to state. Typically, a high school diploma is required (with incentive pay for an undergraduate degree) along with passage of a civil service examination. Training for correctional officers varies widely among the states. Frequently, however, training for new officers consists of a few weeks of classroom instruction.

CORRECTIONAL OFFICER AND INMATE ATTITUDES

Historically, correctional officers, like their police counterparts, have been organized along paramilitary lines and were expected to employ rigorous rule enforcement and coercion to maintain institutional security. Supervisory officers usually judge their subordinate officers' work performance on the basis of how "quietly" their work assignments are completed, including the absence of any problems regarding an officer's performance. This inherent contradiction of expectations has impressed correctional officers with the attitude that they themselves are very much on their own in terms of job assignments and dealing with inmates. Correctional officers learn quickly that in many respects, they are just as much a captive as the inmate. Correctional officers are significantly outnumbered by inmates and confined in close quarters with them. While correctional officers are usually unarmed, inmates may have ready access to crude but effective homemade weapons. Adding to the feeling of captivity or restrictiveness and proximity to potentially dangerous inmates, correctional officers feel the tension generated by the possibility of major assaults or riots within the prison population (Jacobs and Retsky, 1975). Two studies of correctional officers suggest that a dominant aspect of their work is danger and uncertainty (Guenther, 1976; Jacobs and Retsky, 1975). Nevertheless, correctional officers tend to be dependent upon inmates for successful work performance. This usually requires that the officer gain and maintain inmates' active cooperation. Recognizing this need, offenders expect correctional officers to be reasonable and consistent, and to refrain from engaging in overly strict rule enforcement.

Correctional officers realize they must deal routinely with individuals (some of whom are considered unpredictable and dangerous), whose cooperation they must gain and maintain. Correctional officers' problems are compounded by the fact that they may be called upon to be rehabilitative or treatment personnel in the sense of counseling and assisting inmates, rather than merely serving in a supervisory and enforcement role (May, 1976). However, in recent years, a competing view of criminal behavior based upon utilitarian principles that hold the individual responsible for criminal acts has increased the use of correctional officers as advocates for punishment rather than treatment. Correctional officers have shifted from more treatment-oriented positions to a more get-tough custodial position reflecting public opinion and legislation on crime (Cullen, Lutze, Link, and Wolfe, 1989). One result of this change has been a mixture of correctional officer policies and attitudes. Officers in the system who were trained during the last twenty years when the positivist reform model was at the forefront received training that complemented the rehabilitative ideal. New officers entering the profession are now trained on principles of punishment. This often leaves the correctional force with conflicting attitudes on how to deal with inmates and few precise guidelines.

Correctional officers and inmates tend to hold rather negative, stereotypical views of one another (Chang and Zastrow, 1976). The negativism, danger, and unpredictability that seem to be a pervasive part of correctional officers' perceptions of their work may account for the extremely high rate of turnover among new correctional officers. Inmates tend to view correctional officers in a negative manner because it is part of the role of being an inmate:

> For a prisoner, of course, a guard is possibly the lowest imaginable form of humanoid life, a species somewhere about the level

of the gorilla and often rather easily mistaken for one. He's called a bull, a pig, a wethead or a screw, and it's understood he'd rather shoot you than give you the time of day, stick you in the back rather than give you a crust of bread.... The intriguing aspect of this view of guards, however, is that no inmate I've ever met came by it through his own experience—at least not initially. It's an opinion a prisoner automatically picks up at the door, along with his issue of prison clothes and his government-issue toothbrush, and from that point on he simply looks for incidents to confirm the view. Without even having to discuss it, he understands instinctively that such an opinion goes along with his khaki shirt and his cheapo boots, that it's wise to establish one's loyalties clearly and that guard-hating is an act which clearly confirms such a loyalty to the inmate cause. It's expressly part of the function of being a prisoner. (Schroeder, 1976)

CORRECTIONAL OFFICERS AS COUNSELORS

Typically, correctional institutions have performed more effectively in custodial care (security) than in any other aspect of the institution's correctional programs (May, 1976). The opportunities for correctional officers to use excessive force, the routinization of behavior for inmates, and the focus on custodial care as opposed to treatment create an environment that may be unintentionally detrimental to any rehabilitative efforts. While the official policy of the correctional institution may be humane, correctional officers who are in direct contact with inmates may have a different view of their role. Unfortunately, negative outcomes may often be due to the process whereby custodial care is carried out by those least trained in treatment and/or management techniques (Johnson, 1987). Williamson (1990) has indicated that the dramatic expansion of correctional officers under a more punitive system may constitute a setback in professionalism and opportunities for offender treatment. However, Cullen et al. (1989) found many correctional officers still supported the rehabilitative model and defined their roles as more correcting than guarding.

The relationship between custodial care and treatment has historically been one of opposition. Such a relationship pits custody and treatment personnel against each other. What treatment personnel may attempt to do, security personnel can sometimes destroy and vice-versa. Disciplinary infractions, program scheduling and other custodial considerations can prevent, hamper, or terminate inmate involvement in the institution's treatment programs (e.g., academic, counseling, vocational, etc.).

Treatment-oriented personnel often express concern about the conflict between custodial care and treatment needs. While institutional rules and regulations play a vital role in the correctional process, unnecessary rules and the regimens of daily prison life often impede the development of individual inmate responsibility and the ability to accept treatment.

Despite the stress and tensions correctional officers are faced with, most tend to find a substantial amount of job satisfaction (Hill, 1982; Lindquist and Whitehead, 1986a). Although correctional officers have proven to be the least satisfied workers of all correctional personnel, they are only slightly more dissatisfied with their jobs than are other functional specialists (therapists, counselors, psychologists, etc.) (Joint Commission on Correctional Manpower and Training, 1968; Lindquist and Whitehead, 1986b). When queried in a survey, correctional officers replied that they liked three major factors about their jobs: (1) the opportunity of working with and helping prisoners and their families; (2) the interesting and satisfying nature of the work, which lent a feeling of accomplishment; and (3) the chance of viewing results, or watching improvements (Joint Commission, 1968; Lindquist and Whitehead, 1986b).

Correctional officers are more liberal in their attitudes concerning the purpose of incarceration than most would anticipate. Cullen, et al. (1989) found that many correctional officers felt "rehabilitation" should have primary emphasis in correctional institutions. Only a few correctional officers indicated that "punishment" was the goal of corrections.

Given the recent trend toward a more punitive approach for incarceration, correctional officers seem to hold higher expectations than many academic and professional criminologists about the correctional institution's ability to rehabilitate offenders. Correctional officers, in this respect, are probably underutilized in their interaction with inmates for therapeutic and counseling purposes. Given the proper training and education, correctional officers could be a cost-effective method of providing more structured informal counseling to inmates.

Despite the seemingly liberal viewpoints of correctional officers, there appears to be a continued perception on the part of correctional officers that inmates are not to be treated as citizens (Whitehead and Lindquist, 1989). Criminal acts against inmates by other inmates are rarely reported or taken seriously by correctional security personnel. Violent acts such as robbery, rape, assault and even murder are a part of the inmate's world. While these crimes may make headline news for the general public, such violence against inmates is not generally perceived as serious (Ross, 1981; Braswell and Miller, 1989).

SUMMARY

Over two-thirds of correctional institutional employees are custodial "line workers." This high percentage is the result of traditional views concerning roles, correctional philosophies, and building designs. Unfortunately, it is the same traditional views that relegate the correctional officer to second-class status, both within the criminal justice system and where the public at large is concerned! Although new treatment programs have entered the correctional picture, the emphasis on custody and the lack of trained program and treatment personnel will probably keep this percentage high for years to come.

Both the expectations of society and legal requirements make the custodial role the main function of the correctional system. Correctional administrators cannot ignore this. The control of inmates must be maintained, otherwise treatment programs won't be able to produce effective results. Effective treatment seems to require that offenders be present, be under control, and have an appropriate attitude.

The problem with custodial or security personnel is not the fact that they are necessary, but rather why and how they perform their tasks. Correctional officers are normal people placed in abnormal conditions. When great numbers are to be managed by a limited staff, there must be some means of control. This control has typically taken the form of a paramilitary custody model for correctional security personnel. The paramilitary custody model is not particularly suited for helping or treatment methods. Since correctional officers have more contact with inmates, their roles in treatment may be underutilized. In the past, some professionals have maintained that correctional officers should be trained in counseling skills as well as in security maintenance to further the attempts at resocialization of offenders (May, 1976).

References

Braswell, M. and Miller, L. (1989). The seriousness of inmate induced prison violence: An analysis of correctional personnel perceptions. *Journal of Criminal Justice*, 1989, 17:47–53.

Bureau of Labor Statistics, U.S. Department of Labor. (2005). *Occupational outlook handbook, 2004–05 edition*, correctional officers, on the Internet. Available: http://www.bls.gov/oco/ocos156.htm.

Chang, D. H. and Zastrow, C. H. (1976). Inmates' and security guards' perceptions of themselves and of each other: A comparative study. *International Journal of Criminology and Penology*, 4:89.

Cullen, F., Lutze, F., Link, B., and Wolfe, N. (1989). The correctional orientation of prison guards: Do officers support rehabilitation? *Federal Probation*, 53:33–41.

Fogel, David. (1975). *We are the living proof.* Cincinnati: Anderson Publishing Company.

Guenther, A. L. and Guenther, M. Q. (1975). Screws vs. thugs. In A. L. Guenther (Ed.), *Criminal behavior and social systems,* 2nd ed. Chicago: Rand McNally College Publishing Co.

Hawkins, Gordon. (1976). *Prison: Policy and practice.* Chicago: University of Chicago Press.

Hill, W. R. (1982). Who cares for the keepers: Stress awareness for corrections persons. *Police Stress*, February.

Jacobs, J. and Crotty, N. (1983). The guard's world. In J. Jacobs (Ed.) *New perspectives on prisons and imprisonment.* Ithaca, NY: Cornell University Press.

Jacobs, J. B. and Retsky, H. G. (1975). Prison guard. *Urban Life*, 4:22.

Johnson, R. (1987). *Hard time: Understanding and reforming the prison.* Monterey, CA: Brooks/Cole.

Joint Commission on Correctional Manpower and Training. (1968). *Corrections 1968: A climate for change.* Washington, DC: U.S. Government Printing Office.

Lindquist, C. and Whitehead, J. (1986a). Burnout, job stress and job satisfaction among southern correctional officers: Perceptions and causal factors. *Journal of Offender Counseling, Services and Rehabilitation*, 10:5–26.

———. (1986b). Guards released from prison: A natural experiment in job enlargement. *Journal of Criminal Justice*, 14:283–94.

May, Edgar. (1976). Prison guards in America. *Corrections Magazine*, 2(12):40.

Motivans, J. J. (1963). Occupational socialization and personality: A study of the prison guard. *Proceedings of the annual congress of the American Correctional Association.* Washington, DC: American Correctional Association.

Ross, R. R. (1981). *Prison guard/correctional officer: The use and abuse of the human resources of the prison.* Toronto: Butterworths.

Schroeder, Andreas. (1976). *Shaking it rough.* Garden City, NY: Doubleday.

Weisheit, R. A., Falcone, D. N. and Wells, L. E. (2006). *Crime and policing in rural and small-town America*, 3rd ed. Long Grove, IL: Waveland Press.

Whitehead, J. and Lindquist, C. (1989). Determinants of correctional officer's professional orientation. *Justice Quarterly*, 6:69–87.

Williamson, H. E. (1990). *The corrections profession.* Newbury Park, CA: Sage Publications.

CASE 1

The First Day

You are a twenty-five-year-old correctional officer, and this is your first day on the job. You have recently completed eight weeks of training at the Department of Corrections training academy, where you developed some degree of expertise in such areas as behavior control, self-defense, and general security administration. You have also completed two years of college, earning an Associate of Science degree in Criminal Justice, and you plan to continue studying and to earn a bachelor's degree in the same field.

You have been assigned as an officer on the midnight to 7:00 AM shift in the state prison. This particular prison is a maximum-security institution housing about 2,000 inmates. The facility was originally built in the early 1930s to house no more than 1,200 inmates. Aside from obvious problems created by confining too many inmates in too little space, other factors such as poor lighting and ventilation, long narrow corridors, and fortress-like construction have created a rather depressing and negative atmosphere. Because of your education and academy training, you are confident of your ability to perform your assigned duties in a highly professional manner. You feel that you will be able to communicate well with inmates and prison staff alike. In fact, at the academy you were described as one of the "new breed" of correctional officers—better educated, more understanding, and highly competent.

Upon reporting to work this morning, you went directly to roll call. The shift supervisor informed you that since daily work assignments are distributed on the basis of seniority, you will not choose an assignment but will simply be assigned to duty on a cell block in the special management unit (SMU). The other corrections officers then smile and laugh for no apparent reason. Although you had expected a warmer reception at roll call, you tried to shake it off and accept it as a challenge to prove yourself worthy of the other officers' friendship and respect.

102

Since the supervisor did not bother to inform you where the SMU was located, you had to ask another officer for directions. He pointed you in the general direction and left you with the impression that he was glad it was you going back there rather than him. This officer's lack of concern and his implicit warning added to your growing sense of frustration and caused your confidence to begin to deteriorate. You became nervous about being new on the job and even more uncomfortable because no one seemed to care. The academy instructors taught you how to get along with your fellow officers and display a restrained friendliness toward the inmates, but successfully applying their training was proving to be a very difficult task indeed.

Your first eight-hour tour was, to say the very least, filled with bewilderment and disappointment. While on duty, you tried to start a friendly conversation with the other officer on duty; his only response was, "Don't make no unnecessary enemies." Attempts to introduce yourself and converse with the inmates were even more disappointing. If they spoke at all, it was to describe you in some unflattering terms.

Your first day of work ends with you having second thoughts about your job, what you are supposed to be doing, and your self-worth in general.

Questions for Discussion

It seems apparent that the prison administration in this case is not particularly concerned with helping new officers adjust to the job. If they were concerned, what are some ways they could make new correctional officers' adjustment easier and more meaningful? Would a mentorship program help, where new officers are assigned for a period of time to older and more experienced officers? Even though the administration seems unconcerned, is there anything that you as the new officer can do to more effectively adjust to your job?

CASE 2

A Legacy of Corruption

You are a young woman, born and reared in a rural area in the South. Your family was above average in relation to the working-class families in your town. Your father, a farmer, worked hard and saved his money. As a result he was able to provide you, your brother, two sisters, and your mother with a life of dignity and a sense of belonging—belonging to family, to town, and to country.

There was dignity, but no extras. Work was hard and income uncertain. Thriftiness was no mere virtue; it was a necessity. Your parents imbued you with the "American dream"—that hard work and education would make your life easier and more productive than theirs had been. By education, your parents meant high school and possibly some vocational training.

After high school, you and one of your best friends decided to join the Air Force, enlisting for the full four years. You were assigned to a base in the North, where you were able to learn a profession. Since your Air Force job was in personnel, you planned to seek work in a similar field when you were finally discharged.

When you returned to Midville and your family, you were ready to seek a career and a life of your own. Midville was home to you and you wanted to settle there, but there were no personnel jobs available. You felt that you would like to do something meaningful with your life. You wanted a job that would give you both security and a sense of accomplishment. You even considered reenlistment. Then you saw an advertisement:

> Correctional Officers needed at State Prison. Civil service position, fringe benefits, career opportunity. High school diploma required. Beginning salary $24,000. Apply at personnel office, main prison.

You couldn't believe your eyes! Twenty-four thousand dollars a year! Who could live on that? After several more weeks in a fruitless job search, you decided to apply for a position. You could live at home for awhile, and at least the work would be meaningful.

Six weeks later you completed your basic correctional officers' training, and with your fellow trainees you took and signed your oath of office as provided for in Section 26 of the state code:

> I do solemnly swear or affirm that I will faithfully and diligently perform all the duties required of me as an officer of the Department of Corrections and will observe and execute the laws, rules, and regulations passed and prescribed for the government thereof so far as the same concerns or pertains to my employment; that I will not ill treat or abuse any convict under my care, nor act contrary to the law, rules and regulations prescribed by legal authority, so help me God.

During the three years you have worked at the state prison, you have observed worsening conditions. You have been promoted twice, but your annual gross pay is still only $26,000. The inmate population has increased forty percent, while there has only been a ten percent increase in correctional officer positions. To make matters worse, the political and public mood has become increasingly negative. The education and recreation specialists positions have been eliminated and three of the eight counselor positions have been frozen. No education programs, little if any organized recreation, more inmates, fewer correctional officers, and low power has resulted in dismal working conditions.

Now, to increase your sense of frustration, you have learned that your captain and several other of your fellow officers are taking bribes from inmates in exchange for choice assignments. You mentioned to the captain that word has reached you with regard to the purchased assignments. Instead of being embarrassed or evasive, the captain tells you, "These scumbags would sell their mothers for a dime and they deserve whatever happens to them." He then offers to assign you to the unit in charge of housing so that you can "get in on the action." There are even reports that several of the female officers are earning extra income through having sex with some of the better connected inmates. Since you yourself have been propositioned twice during the last month, you have little doubt that the rumors are true. Conflicting needs flood your consciousness. The last officer to complain about this particular captain was summarily dismissed and threatened with prosecution for possession of contraband which he claimed he was not even aware of. The captain's father is also a former warden of this prison, and his brother is the present business manager of the institution.

Needless to say, the situation has created a major crisis in your life. Your decision will be crucial because of its lasting implications for you. You value your personal integrity and you believe in the intrinsic value of your profession, yet you could use more money. In addition, there is the pragmatic necessity of your employment and your hope for advancement within the system, what there is left of it. You live in a beautiful, if depressed, economic area where few decent jobs exist. What should you do?

Questions for Discussion

In this particular case, should you, as the officer in question, contact someone in the state office rather than the prison superintendent? Or should you initially report your information to the prison internal affairs investigator? What might be the advantages or disadvantages of such a choice? How could the problem you are facing be resolved? How does public and political sentiment directly or indirectly affect the working conditions?

Man in the Middle

The memo from the warden is brief and unmistakably clear:

To all prison personnel:

All fighting, assaults, confrontations, loud arguments, and other contentious interactions between inmates are to be reported in writing at the end of each shift. Participants are to be placed in administrative segregation for not less than forty-eight hours; work assignments are to be changed to less desirable ones; and letters describing each incident will be placed in the inmate's file and with the parole examiner's file. There will be no exceptions.

The Warden

The above letter is the policy statement that you and your fellow officers have just received. The policy clarification is in response to increasing violence within the institution that has resulted in the injury of seven inmates and two officers during the month of July alone.

It is a good memo, supportive of staff, and appropriate at this time because violence between inmates has escalated and needs to be curbed. You are happy that the officer's individual discretion has been removed and that inmates who are put on report will not be able to take you to task for disciplinary action. A penalty is required, and you have no choice.

Your assignment within the institution is the "A" wing, a dormitory unit which consists of special housing for prison aides. Prison aides work irregular shifts, night shifts, or in the hospital and, consequently, are often on call. They are presumed to be more trustworthy— hence, the special housing and more flexible hours. Several of the inmates in this dormitory are administrative and one of them, Browning, probably typed the warden's memo on fighting.

You are working the graveyard shift, 11:00 PM to 7:00 AM. On Tuesday, shortly after midnight, you hear a disturbance and run immediately to the dormitory. From the corridor you turn on the overhead dorm lights. Inside, two inmates are crouched, ready for combat, on opposite sides of a single bed. Both are armed with sharp objects and are slashing at each other as they move from left to right around the bed. The rest of the inmates, though reluctant to get involved, have now seen you. They are divided, with one group enjoying the diversion and wanting the action to continue, and the other group wanting to settle the fight. The combatants are also aware of your presence but continue to circle and glare. You quickly run to the end of the narrow corridor and call for help. Returning to the dorm, you find that the inmates have returned to their respective beds and all weapons have disappeared.

The confrontation is over and you are the only observer. One of the men involved is an aggressive homosexual and former weight-lifter who is head baker for the staff dining room. The other person involved is the head clerk for the chief of prison security. Both offenders are eligible for parole in a few months.

At this point the lieutenant arrives to find no disturbance; instead, he finds the quiet of a hot summer night and you in a state of frustration. "Inmates Smith and Taylor were fighting, sir," you state. "They had weapons. I'll write up the report." The lieutenant ponders a moment. "Well, come on over to the office and let's talk about it." As you approach the office, the lieutenant says, "Look, Steve, you know nothing important happened. Let's not stick our necks out. It's hot. Arguments are bound to happen; it's over now. If you report this, these guys will be denied parole and it'll mean grief for us all." You agree, but point out the recent directive on violence from the warden. "Well, do what you want," the lieutenant says, "but I advise against it."

You are now having difficulty in deciding what to do. If you do not report the incident you will satisfy your lieutenant, who is your immediate supervisor, but you might risk the wrath of the warden. Furthermore, if the warden learns of your failure to report the fight, the lieutenant probably will neither back you nor admit that he advised you to violate the directive. Also, the inmates who know of the directive will know that you deliberately violated a major policy. If you report the incident, you will anger the lieutenant and probably not gain any favor with the warden, since he usually hears only of violations of his directives.

Paradoxically, the warden will more than likely hear of the incident, since all of the inmates in the dormitory work with and for the administrative staff. Grapevine communication in the prison is quite active, and very little goes unnoticed. You also worry about the example you set for the inmates when you do not observe written rules. You wonder if they will lose respect for you if you do not write up the incident.

There is something else to consider. If you do write the report, it is sure to anger some of the inmates, particularly Browning, the clerk who types in the warden's office. Browning is the boyfriend of one of the participants, the weightlifter, and is sure to be angered if his boyfriend loses his parole and his job in the prison bakery. The civilian food-service manager will also be angry, since he will have to train a new bakery chef.

You believe that rules are necessary if there is to be order in the prison. You believe that directives, if legal, should be obeyed consistently and without reservation. If a directive is inappropriate, you believe that it should be challenged openly in a reasonable way. But you also feel that you must try to get along with the people you work with.

You are the man in the middle. No matter what you do, you will upset someone. You must make a decision, even if it is a decision to make no decision.

Questions for Discussion

In this case, the warden's new policy seems to be a good one, yet you could stand to make a number of enemies if you proceed with the report. Should you make an exception with this case, since no one got hurt? What if the same two inmates have another confrontation and one of them is seriously injured? Should you then be held responsible, since you did not write up the initial incident?

CASE 4

A Matter of Discretion

You are assigned as a correctional officer on Cell Block 12, a general-population wing in a maximum-security state prison. The inmates in your block all have assigned jobs and, for the most part, are pretty well behaved. On this particular night, Captain Edwards is the institutional watch commander for the third shift (evening watch, 3–11 PM). Everything has been quiet except for the occasional outbursts of shouting and applause in the inmate dayroom. The seventh and final game of the World Series is on television, and the inmates are avidly watching the hotly contested affair.

Suddenly you realize the time has slipped away as the bell rings, signaling it is "rack down" time—10 PM, lights out. As you enter the dayroom, inmates deluge you with requests to let them stay up until the game is over. It is the bottom of the ninth inning, two outs, a runner on third base, and the home team is down by one run.

You get on your walkie talkie and radio the captain for advice, but he is unable to respond at the moment.

Questions for Discussion

The prison rules about "rack down" times are clear, and your watch commander is a stickler for following the rules. What should you do? Should you exercise your own best judgment and discretion, or should you "play it safe?"

Elder Abuse

You have worked as a correctional officer on the midnight shift at the state prison for the past three years. It has been, at times, a rewarding job that you really enjoy, while at other times there have been incidents that bother you even now. Your relationship with fellow officers is frequently strained, at best. As a college graduate you are suspect to many of them. And you have been admonished by senior officers on a number of occasions to just "get along" and keep your personal views to yourself.

For the past three months you have been assigned to the prison hospital's geriatric unit. For the most part the nurses and officers are professional and treat the inmates with care. These are the most vulnerable inmates—old, infirm, many dying of various illnesses. Still others suffer from various stages of Alzheimer's or senile dementia. There is one elderly inmate in particular who seems to awaken each night, shouting nonsensically, crying out and of course waking up the other inmates as well. Even though the old man is on continuous medication, including one to help him sleep, the nurse frequently withholds the sleeping pill. She and the other officer who works with you have developed an obvious disliking for the old man. One night, immediately after he begins to cry out in his sleep, you start to go to his room, but the other officer tells you that he and the nurse will take care of it. Momentarily you hear the officer shouting at the old man, and then the inmate begins to cry out. After a few moments you decide to check on the continuing racket yourself. As you enter the inmate's room, you see the officer raising his right hand to strike the inmate. The officer has a belt in his hand, and before you can say or do anything, he strikes the inmate in the head with the belt buckle, screaming at him to "shut up." The nurse is holding the feeble old man down so he can offer no resistance.

111

When the officer and nurse notice you standing there, the officer tells you the bruises and marks around the old man's head are a result of him "falling out of bed." The officer glares at you as he instructs you to "mind your own business."

Questions for Discussion

What are some ways the prison administration and treatment staff could help you and other correctional officers feel more confident and better qualified to deal with such situations? Should these situations be reviewed by institution training staff to determine if officers are prepared to deal with such events?

CASE 6

A Riot in the Making?

The correctional supervisor, Sergeant Jackson, is sitting in his cluttered, fly-specked office working a week-old crossword puzzle. Outside his window a black inmate in white coveralls fusses in the garden, snipping and raking, making sure that flower beds are just so. Across from the "Visiting Park," other inmates march toward work areas. A prison runner jogs down the brick street inside the walls; the hundred-year-old live oaks that line the street stand motionless in the still afternoon heat. Elsewhere, the factory noises are beginning to resume following the noon break. The two-way radio crackles in Sergeant Jackson's office, but years of exposure to it have dulled his sensitivity and he no longer notices the radio except when it squawks for him.

This afternoon the Department of Corrections inspection team is scheduled to arrive. They will be accompanied by two newspaper reporters. An ad hoc group of professional and civilian members of the Governor's Prison Reform Committee has been touring the grounds for the past few days, surveying the more glaring inadequacies of the institution and suggesting remedies where possible. Several dormitory units have been quickly painted. Trash has been removed and burned, and there has been a general shakedown and cleanup of cell blocks. Even a new dinner menu has been created to provide more substantial and satisfying meals for the inmates.

The inmates are aware of the impending visit. Some of the more militant ones have been protesting the cleanup on the grounds that the administration is trying to cover up the inadequacies of the institution. Showers, which are usually allowed only once weekly, have been increased to four times a week. Use of medication, such as tranquilizers, has been increased, and some of the inmates regarded as "difficult" have been removed to what is euphemistically called administrative segregation. Overcrowding is a serious problem, as is

113

the quality and frequency of correctional officer training. Still, somehow the system had worked for the last ten years.

Even though Sergeant Jackson's office is less than a showplace, he has straightened it. His clipboard rosters and administrative directives, accumulated in reverse chronological order, hang from hooks instead of lying randomly on whatever flat spot that affords itself. Even as he works his crossword puzzle, he keeps a wary lookout for premature or unexpected official visitors.

"Sergeant Jackson," the radio interrupts, "Sergeant Jackson." The sergeant reaches over, grabs the standing mike, and keys it. "Yeah, Jackson here."

"This is Tolliver. I've got the makings of a problem here. A group from 'E' wing has set up a committee and they want to speak, as a group, to the inspection team this afternoon. I told them I didn't think is was possible, but I said that I would ask you."

"Come on! You know that group of clowns; all they want is a country club. Troublemakers, every one of them. Tell them to forget it!"

"They are pretty insistent, sir."

"You make sure to remind them that the inspectors are only going to be here for a few hours, but we'll be here tomorrow. Remind them how we handled the last inmate protest."

"Okay, I'll tell 'em, but I don't think they will listen."

Sergeant Jackson returned to his crossword puzzle, grumbling to himself about devious inmates always trying to get more than they deserved. Suddenly the radio came alive.

"Sergeant! Sergeant! A group of inmates are moving toward Central Control. They have pipes and appear to be holding three guards as hostages. Do you read?"

Sergeant Jackson grabbed the mike. "Yes, damn it. I read. How many are there? Exactly where are they? Do you have visual contact?" The voice on the other end failed to respond.

Sergeant Jackson looked up from his radio into the scowling faces of armed inmates. Central Control had been taken!

Questions for Discussion

How could Sergeant Jackson have reacted in a different way that might have defused the incident that led to what seems to be a full-scale riot? What are some policies the prison administration could have developed to deal with inmate grievances and other institutional problems that might affect inmates?

A Question of Policy

As a female correctional officer, you have been working at the same women's prison for fifteen years. The inmates call you Marge and respect you as being firm yet fair. You have made some mistakes during your career, but no one has ever questioned your intentions or integrity.

Like anyone working in a prison, you have found that there were some inmates you liked more than others. However, it is rare for you to find an inmate that you cannot work with at all. In fact, you are dedicated to the point that you will often spend some of your own time participating with the female inmates in recreation, arts and crafts, and other cell-block activities.

There is one inmate that you are particularly fond of. She is a young woman about nineteen years of age who is in on a drug offense. Lisa is a shy girl who comes from a broken home. She never had much of a family life; both of her parents had failed in previous marriages. Lisa's drug problems had started in high school when she got mixed up with the wrong crowd. She had felt acceptance by drug groups, and besides, life had seemed easier to cope with while on drugs. Lisa was just beginning to use hard drugs when she got busted. Because she was with a friend who was selling large quantities of drugs, her bust resulted in a trial and a two-year sentence.

While in prison, Lisa has come to you on several occasions with personal problems. Being a first-time offender, she has found prison life very difficult to adjust to. You and she have become good friends in a mutually trusting relationship. On this particular day, however, your relationship has been tested.

Lisa has asked you to mail a personal letter to a close friend who lives in her home town. Since her friend is not a member of her family or her lawyer, his name is not on the approved mailing list. She knows your mailing the letter is a violation of institutional policy, but

115

it is very important to her that she contact her friend just this one time. You know that other correctional officers occasionally mail letters for inmates. You also realize that it would be quite easy for you to mail this particular letter. Still, it is a violation of policy.

If you do not mail the letter, your relationship with Lisa will more than likely deteriorate. If you do mail the letter, you may suffer unanticipated consequences. The decision is going to be a difficult one, and you are going to have to make it.

Questions for Discussion

In this particular case, the inmate simply wants her correctional officer friend to mail a letter to someone who is not on her mailing list. What harm could such a small violation of policy possibly cause? Although other officers occasionally mail letters for inmates, how might such action affect you, who have never done so?

CASE 8

Family Connections

You and another correctional officer, Terry Warner, supervise inmates working in the prison laundry during first shift. Morris Ashton, an inmate serving thirty years for multiple assaults, has pulled you aside and complained about Officer Warner.

Ashton is a brooding, tightly wound inmate who, while quiet and introverted most of the time, has exploded on occasion. Eight months ago he almost killed an inmate who questioned his manhood. During the morning break, he whispers to you that Officer Warner has been playing with a large pocket knife and occasionally taunts him and several other inmates when no one else is around. Policy dictates that the only weapon correctional officers can carry is their nightstick. You also notice that Ashton's hands are shaking when he tells you that if something isn't done, he is afraid of what he might do to the officer in question.

With eight months until your retirement and a full pension, Morris Ashton's complaint is the last thing you want to deal with. Terry Warner is the kind of corrections officer that wouldn't have a job if his cousin was not the head of security. Major Art Warner is everything his bumbling, inept buffoon of a cousin isn't, but cousins are still cousins and, as the old saying goes: "Blood is thicker than water."

Questions for Discussion

The inmate has come to you. Should you report the incident to Major Warner? Will the major believe you or his cousin? Is there anything you can do to cover yourself?

117

The Counselor

Correctional counselors deal with the emotional climate of a correctional environment, attempting to provide inmates with adjustment and rehabilitation counseling services. These services may be rendered on an individual basis or in a group setting.

The following eight cases and text will present you with a variety of professional and personal situations correctional counselors typically find themselves in. Dealing with inmate depression, anger, and deception as well as with the counselor's own sense of frustration are examples of skills required of the correctional counselor. As you react to the cases, consider the feelings of the counselor and the inmate with whom he or she is working.

INTRODUCTION

Correctional or offender counseling involves a variety of mental health and other related helping professionals working with persons who have either informally or formally been identified as delinquent and/or criminal. This area of counseling requires a combination of skill, knowledge, and experience—all of which shape the counselor-therapist's professional attitude and style. Each offender presents the counselor with a new counseling situation and challenge which, in many instances, may offer little promise of an adequate resolution.

The idea of "correctional" counseling may not be compatible with the legitimate interests and purposes of helping offenders. For instance, is the primary goal of counselors who work in prisons one of correcting offenders for successful readjustment to the outside world, or is their primary role more concerned with offenders' adjustment to the institutional world of the prison? Does the basic goal of probation/parole counselors revolve around therapeutically correcting offenders under their supervision, or are they more concerned with case management and the enforcement of the conditions of probation/parole? More fundamentally, one might ask whether or not there is any substantial evidence that counselors could "correct" offenders if they wanted to. What seems to be a more appropriate focus is to view these counselors as helping professionals who attempt to apply their skills and expertise in correctional and related settings. The primary goal of offender counselors and therapists appears to be one of intervening therapeutically with various clients, the majority of whom happen to be offenders. These interventions include prison adjustment, pre-release and post-release vocational and marital/family readjustment, and juvenile problems.

THE COUNSELING PROCESS

Offender counseling and psychotherapy, as with all clinical helping, comprises a process that includes three essential abilities: (1) a sense of timing, (2) effective risking, and (3) a sense of professional humility.

Many counselors and psychotherapists, particularly those who work with offenders, may find it difficult to pay adequate attention to their clients' communication. Perhaps this difficulty is to a large extent the result of the counselor's professional and personal attitude, an attitude that is a reflection of the counselor's dual responsibility (i.e., security and treatment) and the retributive feelings of society in general. In other words, the offender counselor grew up in and came from a social system which is often punishment-oriented in nature. In addition, the counselor who works in a correctional setting is typically concerned, first, with the security/custody needs of the agency and community and second, with the treatment and rehabilitation needs of the offender.

For the counselor to develop a *sense of timing* he or she must be able to respect "where clients are" in terms of their value systems, yet not necessarily respect "what clients have done" in terms of their behavior. Respecting and understanding where the client is helps the counselor have a more accurate perception of the general condition of the offender as well as aids in the implementation of a meaningful treatment strategy. "Listening" is essentially a clinical art that enables the counselor to build a "base" relationship with his or her client, which can increase the potential for positive change to occur. Developing the ability to fully listen to a client requires both patience and perseverance. Giving advice to a client before adequately understanding what they are trying to communicate is like a physician attempting to provide medical treatment before he or she has an adequate idea concerning what the nature of the patient's illness is. Perhaps, in the final analysis, counselors would do well to remember the old adage, "it is not so much 'what' you say as it is 'when' and 'how' you say it."

Effective risking is a skill or an ability that the counselor attempts to impart to his or her client. The offense which brings the client to the counselor could be viewed as a primary "symptom" of other deeper learning and attitudinal conflicts. An important goal of the counseling relationship is to help the offender develop more acceptable ways of relating to his or her environment. Risking in a general sense is not new to many offenders. Every time they have tried to commit a crime, they have risked arrest and possible imprisonment. Risking in a therapeutic sense—in a serious effort to substantially change one's attitude and behavior—is a commitment neither an offender nor a non-offender would take lightly. Such a risk, if unsuccessful, could prove to be devastating to a person's emotional stability and, perhaps, physical survival. For instance, during the era of self-discovery and encounter groups in the 1970s, there were a number of casualties. Individuals experiencing the close intimacy and support of an extended small-group experience occasionally chose to make a radical change in their lives. The changes involved careers, marriages, and other major areas of life. The result of such risks in some cases was emotional illness and even suicide. In other words, problems that have taken a lifetime to evolve rarely can be changed quickly or with a single decision. The key to taking risks is to learn to take risks "effectively." Some offenders often act impulsively without thinking through their actions in terms of what the consequences may be. The counselor should attempt to help the client assess the costs of his or her actions. In other words, if I choose to take a risk, what will it cost me? The costs may be measured in time (e.g., a possible prison sentence), money, more positive or negative relationships, or even life and death.

When evaluating the potential costs of a particular risk, the counselor can help the offender make a more relevant and effective choice by examining three fundamental existential questions: (a) Who am I?; (b) Where am I going?; and (c) Why? These questions provide a counseling focus that is both "here and now" and responsibility-based. "Who am I?" can provide a catalyst for helping clients to put in a better perspective the successes and failures of their past as well as the as yet unrealized hopes and fears of the future in the context of the present—the "here and now." "Where am I going?" suggests two questions: Where do I currently see myself and where do I hope to see myself in the future? This question has particular application in helping offenders with risk-taking regarding vocational and career decisions. "Why?" enables the counselor to help his or her client experience a greater sense of responsibility and accountability for the choices they make and the risks they take. "By fully exploring the "why" of the client's choice, the counselor can help the individual clarify his or her priorities and make a more informed decision in terms of personal meaning and responsibility to others" (Braswell, 1981; p. 12).

Professional humility is the result of one's attitude and, perhaps, of life itself. Experience teaches us that life is not always fair and we cannot always win. Sheldon Kopp (1972) states, "The world is not necessarily just. Being good often does not pay off and there is no compensation for misfortune" (p. 166). In other words, to a large extent life is a "paradoxical" process. Understanding the paradoxical quality of life means that sometimes what seems to be right may, in fact, be wrong and what appears to be wrong may, in fact, be right. Right and wrong may differ simply in degree and be relative to a given context. The counselor cannot really correct a client any more than offenders can be assured that if they make positive socially acceptable decisions, they will be treated fairly. What the counselor and client can both do is to "try" or attempt to make a right or correct choice. The therapeutic context in which such choices can be made is relational.

Relationships form the basis for therapeutic trying of the counselor and offender. One often tries to do the right thing because one wants the respect of parents and friends more than just a good grade in college or a job promotion. The offender will transfer both positive and negative feelings to the counselor as a part of the dynamics of the relationship process. How the counselor responds to these feelings will have a substantial impact on any potential attitude change on the part of the offender.

"Therapeutic intention" is a key quality the counselor attempts to impart to his or her client through modeling and other aspects of the relationship process. In other words, because of his or her sense of humility, the counselor acknowledges that life cannot be controlled. You or I are not free to choose what life brings. Yet, we are free regarding how we choose to try to respond to whatever life brings us. As a result, therapeutic intention concerns the counselor's and/or client's "attempt" to put their good intentions into action. To persevere—to continue trying—is more important to long-term rehabilitation and stability than treatment outcomes or immediate results, since life offers no guarantees for doing the right things. A sense of timing, effective risking, and a sense of humility are qualities that can help persons make positive choices because the attempt itself is a meaningful reward, regardless of the final outcome. In the final analysis, the offender may need the self-respect earned through "trying" to make appropriate choices more than any other correctional benefit the criminal justice system can offer.

TYPES OF OFFENDER COUNSELING

In the broadest sense, the most important counselors for offenders are probably those professionals who intervene with a disruptive individual *before* they become officially designated as an offender by the criminal justice system. Elementary and high school guidance counselors and teachers, in addition to youth camp counselors, are examples of helping professionals who can "make a difference" before, rather than after, the fact in terms of an individual's official contact with the criminal justice system.

Regarding counselors who work with offenders in correctional settings, there are two general categories: (a) community-based and (b) institutional.

Community-based counselors include probation and parole service professionals and halfway-house counselors. Other secondary, yet very important professional resources include mental health centers, employment agencies, volunteers, private helping centers (e.g., alcohol and drug counseling), and pastoral counselors and other church-related resources.

Probation is, perhaps, most utilized as a means of diverting juvenile and adult offenders from correctional institutions. The probation officer/counselor is engaged in a variety of investigative services (e.g., supervision, furlough, work release, presentence, etc.) as well as providing counseling services. Essentially, probation consists of sentencing an offender to a community-based treatment or other correctional program rather than incarcerating the individual. The alternative sentence is subject to certain judicial conditions, including having the offender supervised by the probation agency.

The role of both the probation and parole officer is, to some extent, conflictual in nature. Not only are probation/parole professionals responsible for "supervising" their clients and "enforcing" the conditions of probation or parole, they are also responsible for providing "counseling" and guidance services. The problem centers on the issue of counselor/client "confidentiality." In other words, if the offender is aware that his or her probation/parole officer must investigate and enforce the conditions regarding probation or parole, how confidential a relationship would the client be willing to establish with the probation/parole officer? The confidentiality dilemma of "treatment versus security" is a conflict all offender counselors share. Smykla (1981) has identified an option which could help diminish the treatment/security dilemma: restrict probation/parole professionals so that they function only as "resource" brokers or managers. These managers could attempt to match a probationer or parolee with the most appropriate community resources available (e.g., jobs, housing, health care, etc.). Gardner (1973) lists some basic services that workers in the criminal justice field should be aware of if they are to effectively tap community resources:

1. Home-finding associations: These may aid in the care and placement of children and also offer family assistance and counseling services.

2. Educational institutions: Services that schools may provide in addition to the courses, vocational guidance, testing, etc.

3. Goodwill Industries: Goodwill offers vocational training, counseling, and physical rehabilitation programs to physically handicapped persons, and more recently, to those convicted of crimes.

4. State employment agencies: In addition to job placement, the agencies may work with inmates who are about to be released to the community on parole.

Parole and probation professionals often work closely together in both supervision and treatment of community-based functions. A major difference between the two, needless to say, is the fact that the probation officer usually works with offenders *before* incarceration while the parole officer works with them *after* they have been incarcerated for a period of time. Parole and probation officers are both involved in *revocation* proceedings—a process that responds to violations of the conditions of probation or parole by the offender. While the revocation process for probation is typically channeled through a state or federal district court, revocation proceedings concerning parole violations are processed through a state court or with federal cases, the United States Parole Commission. The results of such proceedings may involve returning the offender to a state or federal prison, or a continuation of probation or parole.

Institutional-based counselors include youth counselors in juvenile correctional institutions and counselors in male and female adult prisons. Ironically, traditional offender treatment philosophy has advocated removing offenders from relatively normal law-abiding community environments to more abnormal, overcrowded, often isolated, prison environments in order to help the offender to learn to become more normal and law-abiding. Needless to say, this treatment philosophy has proven to be somewhat less than successful for rehabilitating offenders. Such a philosophy may serve to satisfy the "retributive" needs of society quite well. However, the question might be asked, how long can our society afford the financial and human costs of this type of philosophy?

To a large extent, institutional counselors are often more involved in "institutional maintenance" than in "offender or correctional treatment." "Keeping the lid on" a prison is of primary concern to administrators, security officers, and treatment professionals alike. This is not to suggest that treatment or rehabilitation never occurs, but such goals are often secondary instead of primary.

TREATMENT CATEGORIES

Three basic categories related to treatment which exist in correctional institutions are: (a) education, (b) recreation, and (c) counseling/casework.

The *educational* specialist working in a prison or the correctional educator in general is confronted with a less than ideal population of potential students. As a group, offenders represent a substantial, if not profound, record of failure. Learning disabilities, negative attitudes, and scarce resources all contribute to a perpetuation of failure and underachievement that was experienced by offenders outside of the prison or training school. Traditional educational approaches simply do not work with most offenders. These persons represent the failures of the typical school environment.

In discussing the need for individualized education, Freasier and White (1983) note that recent studies indicate that 32% of adjudicated juveniles could be classified as learning disabled. They continue by describing factors which have helped inhibit the development and availability of needed special education services for incarcerated and other learning-disabled delinquent youth: (a) lack of cooperation between state and local government, (b) minimal and inadequate educational budgets, and (c) a serious shortage of available special education professionals (p. 27).

Evans (1978) identified six principles essential to establishing an effective inmate education program:

1. Educational activity must be meaningful to the learner.
2. Correctional education must be offered in short, attainable, and measurable segments.
3. There must be reinforcement of learning.
4. There must be balance in the total correctional program in which education is but a part . . . a meaningful part.
5. The institutional educational program must be an accredited one, perhaps even provided by the state educational agency.
6. Above all, there must be a substantial interpersonal relationship established between the teacher and student.

Although not always his or her primary responsibility, the educational specialist in prison may also be involved in vocational/career training and guidance. The Federal Bureau of Prisons developed its vocational programs on the basis of several assumptions: (a) ex-offenders would have a better chance to avoid criminal behavior if they possessed vocational skills enabling them to work at a legitimate job and earn a reasonable income; (b) ex-offenders would be more employable if their vocational training were in job areas for which there was a demand; and (c) appropriate vocational training can be provided through effective management of institutional programs (Allen and Simonsen, 1986). Even in correctional institutions where vocational training resources are severely limited, education and counseling specialists can work within the essential functions to establish training opportunities for offenders. For instance, a prison food services' division can often establish baker, dietician, or other related training programs.

Education, whether it is of an academic or vocational nature, involves relationships. Dennison (1969) suggests that education is basically a process of relationships between students and teachers and between students and other students. Whether the client situation is one of trying to motivate an offender through individualized educational instruction or helping another offender choose a vocation that is both meaningful and marketable, the "relationship" component cannot be underestimated. The counseling and other interpersonal skills the educator brings to his or her relationship with an offender will often prove to determine the margin of success or failure. The best of educational and vocational programs will not work without meaningful and reasonable educator/offender relationships. The converse is also true in that limited program resources can often be overcome as a result of dynamic, positive staff/offender relationships.

The *recreation* specialist in institutional corrections comprises a vital part of both the security and treatment process. Recreation has distinct advantages over other treatment programs. For instance, one does not have to be able to read and write in order to participate in and learn from recreational programs. Even physically disabled offenders can engage in a variety of recreational activities (e.g., arts and crafts, table games). A major problem regarding correctional recreation has been one of perception. Too often, the correctional recreation specialist has been no more than an athletic "coach," coordinating a few recreation experiences such as softball, basketball, and weightlifting which are only meaningful to a small percentage of the inmate population.

The "treatment versus security" dilemma is nowhere more evident than in the area of correctional recreation. If a correctional institution does *not* utilize a varied and comprehensive recreation program, inmates are left with a substantial amount of idle time and very few appropriate outlets to vent any frustrations or tensions they might be experiencing. Such a situation can, of course, result in an increase in physical and emotional conflicts among prisoners ranging from sexual assaults to personal depression. However, if a correctional institution does utilize a varied and comprehensive recreation program, new problems as well as benefits will probably occur. More recreational programs and activities result in a more complex "scheduling" process. Inmate meals, work assignments, education programs and other aspects of institutional life need to operate smoothly in conjunction with recreation activities. Another concern of security would involve *supervision* of recreation events. Inadequate and ineffective supervision could result in a security and treatment nightmare. A lack of or inappropriate supervision of recreation programs would not only undermine the potential treatment value of such activities but could also result in increases in prison violence, escape attempts, and other counterproductive behaviors.

A number of innovations have occurred in recreation and related programming which have implications for corrections. Outward Bound programs have been utilized with juvenile offenders eligible for institutionalization. The programs provide a rugged outdoor experience, usually of one to two weeks in duration, in which the youths engage in (a) physical conditioning (e.g., running, hiking); (b) technical training (e.g., life-saving, solo survival); (c) safety training; and (d) team training (e.g., rescue, firefighting). Exercise as therapy has gained increasing attention with the general public as well as with mental health and correctional treatment programs. Strenuous physical exercise has demonstrated positive psychological benefits for adolescents and for the drug and alcohol addicted (Buffone, 1980). Creative use of institutional libraries and inmate publications has also offered the opportunity for intellectual rather than physical exercise and development.

As far as a correctional counselor is concerned, recreation may well comprise the most important treatment and maintenance component of a correctional institution's programming. Individually and as a group, physically and intellectually, correctional recreation has the potential to help the offender therapeutically more than, perhaps, any other treatment strategy.

Counseling/casework is a "given" skill requirement with any correctional treatment effort. Whether one is an education or recreation specialist or a counselor or caseworker, effective counseling and interpersonal skills are critical. Counseling essentially provides a cohesiveness that enables institutional and other programmatic activities to run as smoothly as possible. Traditionally, counselors work with individual clients and also conduct group counseling sessions relating to different kinds of problems (e.g., drug abuse, sexual offenders, suicide prevention). Formally and more importantly, informally, counselors function as "crisis-interveners." From the newly-arrived first-time offender who is anxious and depressed to the inmate who has just been turned down for parole, the counselor must intervene in a diverse and varied array of interpersonal situations (Masters, 1994). Counselors are to some extent "maintenance-workers"; they try to help offenders adjust and function in the institution with a minimum amount of interpersonal frustration and damage. Effective treatment or rehabilitation does occur, but often only secondarily to general crisis intervention and maintenance functions. Some offenders genuinely want to change, but others do not. Many offenders are comfortable with their criminal careers and engage in counseling as a means of improving their situation in prison and their chances for getting out as soon as possible. Other problems encountered by the offender counselor include: (a) the fact that counseling or therapy is secondary to custody and security concerns, and (b) inmates are generally distrustful or guarded with counselors concerning their vulnerability in disclosing their true feelings (Stevens, 1993).

EFFECTIVENESS OF OFFENDER COUNSELING AND TREATMENT

Whether or not offender counseling is effective depends to a large extent on what meaning one attributes to what is or is not "effective." For some persons, effective counseling and treatment is whatever keeps the prison or training school routine running smoothly with little regard for preparing the offender to return and readjust to the outside community. For others, "effective" treatment programs are equated with whatever programs are "cheapest" to implement and maintain in terms of financial costs. Still other persons, while interested in efficient institutional routine and economy of program costs, are also genuinely concerned with improving the relevancy and accuracy of offender counseling and treatment program evaluations. Regardless of one's perspective, the role, function, and degree of success attributed to offender treatment programs have represented areas of heightened controversy with support ranging from a heavy emphasis on rehabilitation to very little reliance, if any, on offender counseling and treatment programs (Martinson, 1974; Fogel, 1975; Allen, et al., 1985; Wright, 1995; Braswell et al., 2001; Van Voorhis et al., 2004).

Glaser (1971) and, more recently, Coulson and Nutbrown (1992) have offered practical suggestions for correctional administrators, which address administrative concerns as well as treatment needs from an evaluation perspective:

1. Procure the most complete post-release information obtainable on offenders in your custody or under your supervision, and work to make this information more complete.

2. Focus presentation of post-release data on the responsibilities the correctional agency must meet especially on cost-effectiveness.

3. Correctional improvement proposals will be most readily supported if they are introduced piecemeal and include procedures for measuring effectiveness.

The effectiveness of correctional counseling as a rehabilitative tool has come under criticism in recent years. With the emergence of more punitive attitudes toward offenders by legislators and correctional administrators, rehabilitation ideology has been pushed out of the picture in many correctional institutions (Palmer, 1992; Quinn, 2003). However, many scholars argue that rehabilitative treatment in the form of offender counseling is effective and should continue to operate as a high-level priority in correctional facilities (Wright, 1995; Losel, 1993). Cullen (1990) reported that, in a public survey, most people supported a rehabilitative model as opposed to a punitive model for correctional treatment. Citizens generally felt that time in prison should not be wasted, nor should prisons be warehouses or places that inflict pain without clear purpose. Instead, most citizens felt inmates should be provided with the education, training, employment experiences and counseling to enable them to become productive citizens.

Regardless of whether or not one feels offender counseling and treatment has been effective, current police, methodological, economic and evaluation problems are making it necessary for treatment programs and, indeed, all correctional programs, to become increasingly accountable and cost effective.

In conclusion, an attempt to define offender counseling and psychotherapy would include several elements: (a) a clear clinical/professional identity in which some counselors or therapists happen to work primarily with human beings who happen to be offenders; (b) the ability to effectively incorporate and communicate the helping skills of timing, risking, and maintaining professional humility; and finally (c) the capacity for maintaining the perspective of "therapeutic intention"—that one's helping attitude and efforts in a sustained, persevering manner may be more important than measured outcomes such as recidivism rates (Kratcoski, 2004).

Summary

Correctional counseling involves therapeutic intervention with offenders. The primary interventions include prison adjustment, pre- and post-release vocational and social readjustment, and juvenile problems. The effective correctional counselor must possess three essential abilities: (1) a sense of timing, (2) effective risk taking, and (3) a sense of professional humility. These therapeutic abilities help impart to the offender, through modeling and other forms of counselor-client relationships, that appropriate choices in life can be made. The most important counseling is preventive in nature. Offender counselors have the greatest chance of preventing criminality before an offender becomes officially designated as an offender by the criminal justice system. Of the two basic types of correctional counseling (community-based and institutionally based), community-based correctional counseling appears to be the most effective. The nature and environment of correctional institutions often prohibit effective counseling concerning an offender's return to a "normal" society. In addition, institutionally based correctional counseling often takes on the form of maintenance and coping within the institution, rather than preparing an offender for a return to society. There are three basic categories related to treatment which exist in correctional institutions: (1) education, (2) recreation, and (3) counseling/casework. Institutional education programs offer "teacher-student" relationships which may enhance an offender's ability to succeed on the "outside." Recreation also involves relationships which may impart "rules of the game" to "rules for living" for an offender. Counseling/casework involves crisis intervention help for offenders. The counselor, in this sense, is attempting to help the offender adjust to the institutional environment and other related interpersonal problems.

The effectiveness of correctional counseling depends upon what is defined as effective. Some maintain that effective counseling is that which is the most economical and functional in terms of routine handling of offender-institutional problems. Others maintain that effective counseling is that which adequately prepares an offender for release into society. An attempt to define correctional counseling would include: (1) a clear clinical/professional identity; (2) effective use of timing, risking, and humility in a helping sense; and (3) therapeutic intentions, where the helping attitude and efforts of the counselor may be more important than traditional measurements of success (e.g., recidivism rates).

References

Allen, H. et al. (1985). *Probation and parole in America.* New York: The Free Press.

Allen, H. and Simonsen, C. (1986). *Corrections in America.* New York: Macmillan.

Braswell, M. (1981). Existential dimensions of traditional counseling and psychotherapy. *Pennsylvania Journal of Counseling*, 1:12.

Braswell, M., Fuller, J. and Lozoff, B. (2001). *Corrections, peacemaking and restorative justice.* Cincinnati: Anderson Publishing Co.

Buffone, G. (1980). Exercise as therapy. *Journal of Counseling and Psychotherapy*, 3:101–17.

Coulson, G. and Nutbrown, V. (1992). Properties of an ideal rehabilitative program for high need offenders. *International Journal of Offender Therapy and Comparative Criminology* 36(3):203–8.

Cullen, F. (1990). Public support for correctional treatment: The tenacity of rehabilitative ideology. *Criminal Justice and Behavior* 17(1):6–18.

Cullen, F. and Gilbert, K. (1982). *Reaffirming rehabilitation.* Cincinnati: Anderson Publishing Co.

Dennison, G. (1969). *The lives of children.* New York: Random House.

Fogel, D. (1975). *We are the living proof. . . .* Cincinnati: Anderson Publishing Co.

Freasier, A. and White, T. (1983). IEP communicators. *Journal of Correctional Education*, (34):27–29.

Gardner, G. (1973). Community resources: Tools for the correctional agent. *Crime and Delinquency*, 19:54–60.

Glaser, D. (1971). Five practical research suggestions for correctional administrators. *Crime and Delinquency*, January:32–40.

Kopp, S. (1972). *If you meet the buddha on the road, kill him.* Palo Alto, CA: Science and Behavior Books.

Kratcoski, P. (2004). *Correctional counseling and treatment*, 5th ed. Long Grove, IL: Waveland Press.

Losel, F. (1993). The effectiveness of treatment in institutional and community settings. *Criminal Behavior and Mental Health* 3(4):416–37.

Martinson, R. (1974). What works? Questions and answers about prison reform. *The Public Interest,* Spring:22–25.

Masters, R. (1994). *Counseling criminal justice offenders.* Thousand Oaks, CA: Sage Publications.

Smykla, J. (1981). *Community-based corrections: Principles and practices.* New York: Macmillan Publishing Co.

Stevens, G. F. (1993). Inmate behavior dynamics. *Journal of Offender Rehabilitation* 19:1–192.

Wright, R. (1995). Rehabilitation affirmed, rejected, and reaffirmed: Assessments of the effectiveness of offender treatment programs in criminology textbooks. *Journal of Criminal Justice Education* 6(1):21–39.

CASE 1

Wet Behind the Ears

Four years at the university studying corrections and sociology have finally paid off. You have landed your first job as a correctional counselor in a medium-sized prison. Although you do not have any previous work experience, you were an A and B student in school and did especially well during your internship. After arranging your new office to your taste, you prepared yourself for becoming a dynamic part of the rehabilitation process.

At the beginning of the work day you met with the other counselors and your supervisor for coffee and the day's caseload assignments. You were somewhat puzzled at the mixture of amused and disinterested stories that greeted your remarks on the latest research and theory concerning the practice of correctional counseling and treatment. As the day wore on, you became even more perplexed. The security officers escorting your inmate clients were always at least fifteen minutes late. Two of your clients did not even come for counseling; one, who was illiterate, wanted you to read a letter for him from home, and another one wanted you to help him complete some kind of "leather work" kit order form. To make matters worse, you noticed that two of the other counselors worked with only one client each during the entire morning, while you took four different clients. The two counselors spent most of their morning drinking coffee and "shooting the breeze" with each other in one of the offices.

After lunch everything seemed to slow down even more. You could not even get one of your scheduled clients in to see you at all. When you discussed the problem with the security officer responsible for escorting your client, he turned to you and replied, "I got more important things to do than to escort convicts all day." Then, without another word, he abruptly walked away before you even had a chance to reply.

Later that afternoon you had the chance to talk to two of the more experienced counselors, Ned and Julie.

Julie had recently completed her master's degree in counseling. She was clearly hard working and ambitious. Her advice to you was succinct and to the point. "Do you want to become a burned-out malcontent like some of these other counselors, or do you want to get ahead? It's all in the paperwork. I do more case files than anyone else, and I constantly network with people who can help my career. You do the same and you will move right up the ladder of success. If you don't, you will be stuck here like the rest of them."

Ned, in his mid-fifties, lit up his favorite pipe and propped his feet up on the table. He asked you about your family. Every time you mentioned one of the problems you had observed, he just smiled. As you got up to leave, he offered you some parting advice: "Luke, you need to lighten up a little, do what you can to help, and let the rest go. Give yourself a little more time on the job before you decide what's what."

The end of your first working week finds you tired and confused. Most of the other counselors don't seem to care about rehabilitation or any of the other things they were taught in college. They all have behavioral science degrees. What has happened to them? Will the same thing happen to you? Your supervisor also told you to take it easy and give the others a chance to get to know you. Is a career in corrections right for you, or was your choice a mistake?

Questions for Discussion

Are you experiencing the normal frustration of adjusting from the university to an actual work setting? Are you expecting too much, too soon, or are the other more experienced counselors too "used" to their jobs? Should you be more interested in career advancement, or can there be a balance between a career and simply helping?

CASE 2

Confidentiality or Security?

You have been working as a counselor at the community correctional center for three years. You feel good about your job and the results you have achieved. No inmate or civilian has ever questioned Wes Brown's ethics or integrity.

You are presently working on an especially interesting case. A young twenty-two-year-old second-time drug offender named Ted has really been opening up to you and seems to be turning himself around in terms of his personal values and motivation. The trust between the two of you is apparent. In fact, just several days ago the superintendent commented on how much better your client seemed to be doing since you had taken him on your caseload. However, during the last counseling session your client disclosed something that could severely disrupt your relationship with him, and you are not sure what to do about it.

Halfway through your last session, in a moment of frustration, Ted blurted the whole thing out. Apparently he and two other inmates had been planning an escape for some time. After Ted became your client and began making progress, he had second thoughts about being involved in the escape. The other two inmates, however, threatened to implicate him if anything went wrong with their attempt. The escape attempt is planned for the following night. Ted is distraught as to what he should do, and since you are his counselor, you are somewhat distraught also.

As a correctional counselor you are not only responsible for counseling inmates but have implicit security responsibilities as well. If the escape attempt is allowed to continue as planned, correctional officers, inmates, or both might be seriously injured or killed. If the plan is quashed, you will have failed to honor the confidentiality of your client, and Ted will most probably suffer repercussions. Needless to say, your counseling relationship with him will also be severely damaged.

It seems you have to sacrifice either Ted, and your counseling relationship with him, or the security of the correctional center. Confidentiality or security, which must it be? Can there be another way?

Questions for Discussion

Should you inform Ted that you are professionally bound to tell the superintendent about the escape plans, while still attempting to work with Ted? Should you remain silent, hoping that the escape attempt will be unsuccessful and that no one will be injured? Should you go to the superintendent and discreetly attempt to thwart the escape attempt without letting Ted know of your actions?

A Captive Audience?

You have been assigned as the head chaplain at a large state prison for men. One of your many duties is to coordinate a busy schedule of religious programs and activities. You have many lay volunteers who willingly give their time to provide religious programming to the nearly 2,000 men who are incarcerated there. Over the years you have developed and refined an excellent orientation and in-service training regimen for the lay volunteers. While you value their generosity, commitment, and enthusiasm, you also know that otherwise well-intentioned but naïve people can be easily manipulated by inmates. On the other hand, you are also mindful of your obligation to look out for the religious needs and best interests of the inmates as well. There are those few lay volunteers whose fervor and tenacity can be come problematic. While you want dedicated and enthusiastic volunteers, you do not want people who are blindly driven to convert others to their way of thinking. Inmates are, after all, captive audiences.

These concerns always lead you to caution religious volunteers against pressuring inmates to participate in services or study classes, or to be baptized into, join, or otherwise become actively engaged in any particular religious program.

This direct and frank approach has always seemed to work well until now. You were called to the warden's office this morning and told that the governor's office had received complaints from several volunteers that you were discriminating against their church group and discouraging inmates from participating in programs. The governor's directive is clear—stop messing with these fine people!

Questions for Discussion

While most church and religious groups work effectively within prison rules, this church group has been a problem on a number of occasions, with inmates complaining about their "high pressure" tactics. How do you accommodate the governor's instructions yet still protect the inmates from unwanted intrusions by this particular group?

The Group

Ever since you earned your master's degree in social work, you have focused your counseling interests and skills on the group process. You even had a couple of articles published describing your group counseling efforts at the community-based halfway house where you are presently employed. Group work, in your opinion, is the best way to help people solve their problems. It is economical and efficient; you can see ten clients in a group during an hour, while in individual counseling you can see only one person at a time. Of course, you realize that individual counseling is necessary at times. Nevertheless, the group approach is usually better because it requires the group members to interact with each other rather than only with the counselor.

You have utilized the encounter-group process quite effectively on several occasions in the past with juvenile drug offenders. Confrontation seems to be particularly effective in dealing with the "conning" behaviors of many drug users. This approach also seems well suited to your personality as a therapist; no one has ever accused you of being nonassertive when dealing with a client.

Working with your most recent group, however, is proving to be a perplexing and frustrating experience. What began as a typical group of juvenile offenders engaged in open confrontation has degenerated into intimidation and thinly disguised threats. You have even heard rumors that some threats are being made outside the group. You realize you are losing control of the group but are not sure what to do about it. Now you have heard that two of the prison gangs who have members in the group have exchanged unpleasantries over what was said during one of the meetings. At the same time, two or three of the group members have made a lot of progress in accepting responsibility for their problems.

You do not want to admit defeat. You have never lost a group. Yet, confidentiality and adhering to the group's ground rules are essential if trust is to be developed and maintained. You are going to schedule one more meeting in an effort to clear the air and get the group back on track. What will you say? What will you do?

Questions for Discussion

What are your options in this situation? While you are concerned about the needs of the group members, does some concern about your own "track record" enter into the equation?

CASE 5

The Despairing Client

Dave has been in prison for two years. He is a likable inmate who works in the prison library. Dave has a remarkable talent for repairing damaged books. He has saved the library hundreds of dollars with his handiwork.

As his counselor, you try to see him at least once a month to find out how he is getting along. He always indicates that he is doing all right and that he is optimistic regarding his parole hearing, which is only nine months away. Dave has some reason to feel good about his chances for making parole. He is a first-time offender who got into a drunken brawl at a tavern and seriously injured another man. As a result of the altercation, he was sentenced to six years in the state penitentiary. Although Dave had experienced severe drinking problems for a number of years, fighting had never been a part of the problem. Since being in prison, he has joined Alcoholics Anonymous and even successfully completed several college-level courses in library science. Needless to say, counseling Dave is a pleasant experience mostly because of his own motivation.

However, in the last several weeks Dave's behavior and attitude have changed. His wife, who has been visiting him faithfully every Sunday, has not shown up for the last two visitation days. Cell-house rumor is that she has begun seeing another man and is planning to file for a divorce. To make matters worse, the man she is involved with is an alcoholic himself. Dave has quit coming to work and keeps to himself in the cell house. He has also been losing weight and looks haggard and distraught.

As his counselor you want to help, but Dave, who has always been quiet, has now become even more withdrawn. You are not sure how to approach him. You have considered talking to his wife or his parents. If Dave's depression continues to worsen, his behavior may become unpredictable. He might become aggressive and get into a fight with someone in the cell house, or he might turn his anger inward and attempt suicide. You have to approach him, but how? You have to do something in an attempt to help him, but what?

Questions for Discussion

Dave's wife's decision to sue for divorce has affected him adversely. You want to help Dave, but is this possible? Can you help bring Dave and his wife back together? Can you help Dave reconcile himself to his wife's decision? What could you have done before the problems escalated into a divorce situation?

CASE 6

Dealing with Anger

You have been a counselor for ten years, but this is one part of your job that has never gotten any easier.

Doug, an inmate at the institution where you work, has just been turned down for parole for the second time in six years. The two of you are sitting at the hearing-room table, quietly staring out the barred window. You can see the tears silently streaming down Doug's face. You can sense the anger and humiliation he is feeling and the explosion within himself that he is fighting to contain.

Doug has a good prison record with respect to both his conduct and his commitment to rehabilitation programs. The problem is apparently a political one. The local judge simply does not want Doug released in his county. As the institutional counselor, you know of several other inmates who have been granted parole to that particular county. They were paroled despite their having committed more serious offenses than Doug and having been much less receptive to the various institutional rehabilitation programs. Doug also knows of these paroles. To make matters worse, the parole board did not even give him a reason for rejecting his application, nor did they tell him what he could do to increase his chances for parole in the future.

Doug spent weeks in preparation for his parole hearing. The letters of recommendation, the acquisition of his high school diploma, and other related material had in the end meant nothing. The board had convened less than ten minutes to make a parole decision based on six years of Doug's life. The chairman simply told you that Doug's parole had been denied and for you to pass the decision along to Doug. You had reluctantly done so, knowing that Doug could see the decision in your eyes before you even spoke. So here the two of you sit, bitter and disillusioned.

Will Doug give up? Will his anger get him into trouble with the administration or other inmates in the cell house? How will this affect your relationship with him, since you were the one who encouraged him to apply? You are not sure what to do or say, but somehow you have to try to help Doug pick up the pieces.

Questions for Discussion

Even though the parole denial in this particular case might have been politically motivated, how could the "hearing" have been better handled? Is there anything else the you can do that might improve Doug's chances at the next hearing?

CASE 7

Counseling a Hostage Victim

"Doc, I've been a corrections officer for 15 years. I've always looked forward to coming to work. But since I was taken hostage eight weeks ago, I'm not sure I can do my job anymore. I'm ashamed to admit it, but I'm afraid. I know me, Buddy, and Sam were only held by the inmates in C block for 48 hours, but I've been having problems ever since."

As the prison psychologist and a licensed therapist, you assure Ted that you understand and encourage him to continue.

"The thing that bothers me the most was seeing that young inmate raped by those three sons-of-bitches and not being able to help him. Every time I think about it. . . ." Ted stops talking and bows his head, quickly wiping a tear from the corner of his eye.

"Ted, go ahead. Let your feelings out. I would have been angry and scared, too. It's a tough thing to have to go through," you reply.

"Doc, it's worse than tough. Good lord, that young man is only twenty-three with a wife and baby. I haven't had a good night's sleep since this thing happened. And Buddy and Sam's done quit. Buddy's wife doesn't even know where he is. I want to go back to work, but my wife says I should quit and find something safer to do. The only thing I have ever done is corrections. I just don't know what to do. What do you think I should do, Doc?"

You look thoughtfully at Ted and rub your chin, wondering how you should respond. He needs to face his fears, but he and his family also need to have a life again. Ted is waiting for your opinion.

Questions for Discussion

Being the victim of a hostage incident can be very traumatic. Whether a correctional officer or an inmate, witnessing a rape or being raped is very disturbing and frightening. What are some relationship problems Ted may be experiencing? What are some different options within the prison that could ease Ted back into his work routine? Should his wife be included in your counseling sessions with him? Should he be referred to outside mental health professionals? Does the prison have an employee assistance program in place to deal with such situations?

Suicide by Counselor

Your institution has a treatment program for inmates who are identified as sexual predators. Once identified, these inmates are placed in isolation in a maximum-security setting for 90 days. If they incur no disciplinary violations during that time, they are reviewed by the classification team and released back into the general population.

Inmate George Smith received a rule violation for breaking prison rules regarding unacceptable sexual behavior. Smith has served his 90 days in isolation without receiving any write-ups for rules infractions. When he meets the classification committee, he is approved for release back into the general population. However, his caseworker, who works in an office next to yours, decided to leave him in isolation because she personally dislikes him. Five days later, after repeated unsuccessful requests to see his caseworker, Smith hangs himself in his cell. He leaves a note saying he can't understand why he's not being allowed to get out of isolation. The deputy superintendent in charge of treatment is meeting with each of the caseworkers to investigate the note and circumstances surrounding George Smith's death. You are scheduled to meet with the deputy warden first thing in the morning.

Questions for Discussion

Was this tragedy avoidable? Did the George Smith's caseworker act ethically or professionally? What are you going to tell the deputy superintendent when you meet with him? What do you think the outcome of this situation should be?

Correctional Ethics

Ethics involves a wide range of discretionary decision making affected by philosophical, social, and political factors. The eight cases and text in this section deal with a number of ethical dilemmas you may be confronted with in the correctional system. As you react to the cases, try to determine how your decisions are affected by your own personal values and the social and political environment. You should also try to determine how your decisions will affect those around you.

INTRODUCTION

In recent years much has been written and spoken concerning the topic of ethics. Frequently one hears of political decisions and ethics, governmental actions and ethics, or ethical considerations that occur within everyday social events. Still, many people do not seem to have an accurate sense of what the term ethics means. Webster defines ethics as:

> . . . a particular system of principles and rules concerning duty, whether true or false; rules of practice in respect to a single class of human actions. . . .

Using this definition, ethics could mean many things to many people, according to how it is applied. In essence, however, one could suggest that ethics is "the science of human duty." In addition, when applied in a concrete moral context, doing one's duty could also mean doing what is "right," regardless of the cost to oneself or others.

Members of society have a duty to both themselves and other members within that society to maintain certain rules and principles. Statutes and laws, as imperfect as they may be, are derived from these principles and rules and are what our legal system is based upon.

Ethics comprise the fundamental framework for how an individual lives his or her life and exists within society. Everyone has within themselves their own personal ethical framework, and at times their ethical observation of a given situation will differ from someone else's. That is why there are often controversial issues such as abortion and capital punishment, because what one person perceives as an unethical approach to a given situation may seem perfectly appropriate to someone else.

Ethics within the realm of corrections can be very difficult to understand, since many of us often feel that when someone breaks the law and is sentenced to spend time in a correctional facility, he or she gives up certain rights and privileges that exist within a free society. In some instances to some people, the forfeiture of these rights and privileges may seem extreme and uncalled for, even unethical. Still other persons may believe that legal sanctions should be even more severe. Following is an examination of some of the ethical considerations that exist within the correctional process.

EVOLUTION OF PRISONERS' RIGHTS

In the late 1960s and the decades of the 1970s and 1980s, the courts embraced a new jurisprudence by rethinking the long tradition of not interfering in the management of penal affairs of the state, a tradition based on federalism and the common law theory of legal death of convicts. This tradition was known as the "hands-off doctrine" (*Banning v. Looney*, 1954). A restated "hands-off" doctrine that recognized and affirmed the civil rights of prisoners through court decisions became the focal point of litigation aimed at penal institutions. It coincided with the mood of the country to affirm the viability of the civil rights movement in all walks of life (*Washington v. Lee*, 1968). Correctional issues involving freedom of religion, safety, medical care, housing, mail, and the rights of juveniles were a few of the issues that were addressed by the courts. More recently, the courts revisited the restated "hands-off" doctrine and have exercised restraint in its further expansion (*Baker v. Holden*, 1992). Congress visited the prisoner rights issue in 1995 with passage of the Prison Litigation Reform Act, which among other things mandated a requirement that inmates exhaust administrative remedies prior to filing lawsuits regarding prison conditions.

Apparently, the courts have recognized the enormous complexity and interrelationships of issues such as overcrowding that involve changing social values and economics, realities that prison administrators and local governments face each day. It is a judicial balancing act in which the court balances the new recognition of civil rights of convicts with the ability of local government and prison authorities to maintain security, safety, and discipline within the prisons.

Almost every facet of prison life and administration is encompassed by some form of ethical consideration. Whenever the Supreme Court hands down decisions regarding prisoners' rights,

Table 1   Prisoners' Rights

1. *Shack v. Wainwright* (1967) held that censorship of mail does not violate an inmate's First Amendment right; however, censorship of letters to and from attorneys or government agencies was held in *Taylor v. Sterret* (1976) to be unreasonable. *Pepperling v. Crist* (1984) holds that prohibition of prisoners' receipt of "sexually explicit" material is an infringement of First Amendment rights. The court further defined censorship of inmate mail in *Thornburg v. Abbott* (1989) by holding that incoming mail may be rejected if it is found to be a detriment to the security, good order, or discipline of the institution, or if it could facilitate criminal activity.

2. *Cruz v. Beto* (1971) held that inmates may exercise fully their religious beliefs as long as the practices of a particular faith do not violate prison regulations. In *Bone v. Commissioner of Prisons* (1994) the court allowed a prisoner in disciplinary confinement to pray and read religious texts.

3. *Johnson v. Avery* (1969) held that an inmate has the right to receive legal aid from another prisoner. In *Procunier v. Martinez* (1974) the court held that inmates are entitled to file their grievances with the court. *Bounds v. Smith* (1976) held that inmates must have access to law libraries when there is an absence of adequate direct legal assistance. In *Miller v. Evans* (1992) the court held that inmates at other facilities were to be given transportation and housing to prisons with law libraries, if necessary, to allow for a full day of research.

4. *Newman v. Alabama* (1977) held that inmates have a right to visitation privileges on a regular basis. *Mary of Oakknoll v. Coughlin* (1985) held that conjugal visits are permitted at the discretion of the prison administration if allowed by the legislature.

5. *Parnell v. Waldrep* (1984) held that correctional facilities that do not provide proper physical exercise and recreation violate the prisoner's constitutional rights.

6. *Hudson v. Palmer* (1984) held that an inmate does not have a right to privacy due to the objective of a prison, but a prisoner's personal property is protected from intentional destruction at the hands of prison officials. In *Grummett v. Rushen* (1985) and *Michenfelder v. Summer* (1988) the court held that female correctional officers were entitled to equal opportunity employment, and that pat-down searches were allowed on male inmates by female guards. In *Canedy v. Boardman* (1992) the court held that women correctional officers could conduct cross-gender strip searches in a professional manner and not violate an inmate's right to privacy.

7. *Howard v. Wheaton* (1987) held that there were restrictions on the use of solitary confinement. *Young v. Quinlan* (1992) held that the overriding issue in solitary confinement was the physical health and/or mental health of the inmate.

8. *Walsh v. Mellas* (1988) held that precautions should be taken in assignment of cell mates due mainly to gang-related violence.

9. *Washington v. Lee* (1968) affirmed the decision of the lower court that ordered the prisons to desegregate.

10. *Rhodes v. Chapman* (1982) held that overcrowding *per se* is not necessarily a condition that violates the Eighth Amendment. To be cruel and unusual there must be wanton and unnecessary infliction of pain, or be a condition that is grossly disproportionate to the severity of the crime warranting punishment. The fact that overcrowding falls below contemporary standards does not make the overcrowding unconstitutional.

11. *Estelle v. Gamble* (1976) held that medical and health care were constitutional rights to prisoners. In *Washington v. Harper* (1990) the Supreme Court held that an inmate could be administered psychiatric drugs if an inmate is dangerous to himself or others.

12. *Porter v. Nussle* (2002) (Prison litigation Reform Act) held that inmates must exhaust all administrative remedies before filing suit in Federal court.

they satisfy some constituents and enrage others. Still, their decisions continue to attempt to maintain a viable balance between the rights of the kept with the duties and needs of the keepers.

PUNISHMENT VERSUS REFORM

An ethical controversy that remains at the forefront in corrections is whether prisons are simply custodial warehouses for lawbreakers or whether these facilities should be treatment oriented, aimed at reforming criminals into productive members of society.

Early correctional facilities were not concerned with rehabilitating offenders, they were only concerned with punishment (Langbein, 1976). In the 1850s society began to view reform as another correctional goal in addition to the existing goal of punishment. Since then, there has been much debate concerning what the true goals of corrections are. Those persons who argue that prisons exist to mete out punishment for offenders tend to believe that treatment doesn't work. Although he later softened his position, Martinson (1974) originally wrote that there is

> . . . very little reason to hope that we have in fact found a sure way of reducing recidivism through rehabilitation . . . instances of rehabilitation have been isolated. . . . (p. 71)

Also, cost is a pervasive issue. Treatment and rehabilitative programs are expensive, and many feel that maintaining prisons cost enough without such an added expense (Vito, 1981).

On the other side, pro-treatment supporters argue that society has a duty to try to rehabilitate offenders so that they can return to and be an active part of society (Sechrest, 1979). They also argue that some type of treatment, no matter how minimal, is better than doing nothing at all.

When addressing treatment issues, another question that inevitably arises is whether treatment should be forced on an individual. Some feel that treatment is viewed by inmates as a coercive type of punishment (Wilkins, 1969). A number of professionals feel that although inmates do have to live under certain restrictions and regulations, they should still have some amount of free choice to live as they want within the guidelines of prison rules and sanctions. Other professionals believe that given the potential benefits of rehabilitation and reform, coercive treatment can be justified.

OVERCROWDING

Overcrowding is a problem in corrections because at some point it becomes unconstitutional (*Rhodes v. Chapman*, 1981) and a violation of the prisoner's Eighth Amendment rights. It is self-perpetuating by a philosophical notion that prison is the appropriate punishment for almost all criminal offenses. Overcrowding is a problem because it gives birth to hard ethical problems such as prisoner victimization by other prisoners and unlawful conduct by custodial officers, including brutality, extortion, and graft. It creates a feeling of frustration and helplessness throughout the staff, robbing them of the energy and motivation to bring about creative changes. It is no wonder that overcrowding is recognized as the most pressing problem in corrections today.

Overcrowding becomes a constitutional issue when it inflicts wanton or unnecessary pain or is excessive to the severity of the crime committed (*Coker v. Georgia*, 1977). Overcrowding is not just an issue of numbers and space but is also a cause-and-effect relationship of numbers, space, and resulting events. For example, double bunking two persons in a one-person cell is overcrowded but not unconstitutional (*Rhodes v. Chapman*, 1981), but double bunking two in a cell designed for one may be unconstitutional when the cell mates are from rival gangs (*Walsh v. Mellas*, 1988).

Given this standard, it would appear that jails would be the most vulnerable to constitutional issues arising from overcrowding because they house mostly pre-trial detainees and misdemeanants. A higher standard of care is thus required because of the lesser severity of the crime, and in the case of pre-trial detainees, perhaps no crime at all. But jails seem to be coping with their problems of overcrowding, partly because of the infusion of federal funds into local jail facilities, and partly because grassroots politics in the communities have brought pressure on state government to move prisoners sentenced to terms of one year or more quickly out of local facilities and into state penitentiaries. Federally mandated jail capacity certifications reinforced this process. Local governments have also pressured district attorneys into seeking quicker indictments and trial dates, as well as limiting pre-trial detention and jail time for misdemeanants instead of fines. These remedial measures are not available to the state department of corrections. While overcrowding still threatens the jails, the Bureau of Justice Statistics (1996) show jail populations within the last ten years as averaging out at about 90% capacity, consistently under levels of overcrowding.

With the jails no longer a tidal basin to catch the overflow of state prisoners, the only options left to the state are to expand and build, to contract with the private sector or contract with the counties (if they are agreeable), to develop new community programs, to revise parole eligibility, and for the governor to exercise his powers of executive clemency.

The federal government has shown no reluctance to force changes in state corrections systems and to order measures to reduce unconstitutional crowding. In *Gates v. Collier* (1971), the U.S. District Court of the Northern District of Mississippi ordered changes in the state penitentiary and capacities assigned to the state jails. They virtually became an agent of oversight of penitentiary operations (Taylor, 1993).

Elimination of unlawful overcrowding and other unconstitutional conditions will not be solved in the long run by the state taking over county jails, or by the federal government taking over state correctional systems. It will be solved in a change in the way in which the community views their correctional problems. Just as the community has come to recognize the need for dedicated public school teachers and new school facilities, a new community standard must evolve in which the community more carefully matches the punishment with the crime and is willing to accept the financial responsibility to carry it out in a way that extends the American civil rights tradition to those incarcerated.

VIOLENCE

Confinement in cramped quarters, men with histories of engaging in violent interpersonal acts, restriction of movement and behavior, allowing no contact with women, and being constantly monitored—all contribute to violence (Cole, 1988). Each year more than one hundred inmates die, and countless more are injured through assaults and suicides.

In 1980, *Walsh v. Brewer,* the Supreme Court decided that inmates have a right to be reasonably protected from constant threats of violence and sexual assaults. However, such a ruling is much easier written than implemented. The conditions previously mentioned, when compounded with one another, often lead to frequent and severe violence. Prison staff and administration are confronted daily with ordeals of assaults and violence, and the problem continues to escalate in some prisons. Prison gangs and racism also contribute substantially to the problem. New solutions are constantly being sought, but none of yet have led to a drastic decrease in violence. Following are some examples of attempts by prison officials to decrease acts of violence.

Overcrowding is believed to greatly enhance the probability of violence (Ingraham and Wellford, 1987). To combat overcrowding early-release programs have been enacted, parole processes expedited, more prisons constructed, and neighboring states' prison facilities used (Mullen, 1987). Although these programs have helped somewhat, no substantial reduction of violence has been noted.

Another tentative solution that has had some positive results involves prison administrators hiring better educated and qualified personnel to supervise prisoners. Such correctional staff and security officers encourage discipline and respect and uphold prison rules and regulations (Fleischer, 1989). More effective pre-service and in-service training can also help diminish officer brutality and increase interpersonal competence.

In the case of sexually related crimes, younger and more vulnerable inmates are being watched more closely and some are being put in protective custody or another cell block (Fleischer, 1989). This is a temporary solution, and many prisoners who are given such special treatment and protection may even be at greater risk when they return to general population. Also, as mentioned earlier, some states now allow conjugal visits with spouses in prison or furlough visits outside of prison. As more states adopt this philosophy, a reduction in sexually related violence can, and hopefully will, be the result.

Ethical issues also arise concerning guards and the force used on inmates. Discipline must be maintained in a prison environment and in a number of instances a strict, forceful type of discipline is in order. Yet there are occasions when too much force is used. Inmates often complain of guard brutality and disregard for their personal well-being (Johnson, 1987). In *Hudson v. Palmer,* the Supreme Court held that discipline must not include "physically barbarous actions" or "unnecessary and wanton infliction of pain." As in the case of prisons providing safety for inmates, the court can set precedent, but the prison officials must see to its adherence, and many times such rulings are not adequately implemented for a variety of reasons. In addition, it is virtually impossible to have complete control over the actions of correctional officers (Sykes, 1956).

PRIVATIZATION OF CORRECTIONAL FACILITIES

Recently a number of privately owned and operated jails and prisons have come into operation in the United States. For many persons, this poses a serious ethical dilemma. First, the question of whether it is right to profit from the misfortune of criminals is debated; and second, problems arise concerning giving the legal authority to administer justice to contracting nongovernmental parties (Dilulio, 1988). Along these lines the debate also centers on the point that convicted criminals are being supervised and treated by civilian profit-oriented organizations. Although privatization of prisons and jails has come under scrutiny, there is also a potentially positive side to consider. Since privately owned correctional facilities are business oriented, they sometimes may be run more efficiently and economically than state and locally run facilities. In addition, the cost of housing inmates is often found to be cheaper, sometimes as much as 20% less than government run facilities (Harms and Allen, 1987). Of course, quality versus economy is a hotly debated issue concerning such cost-effectiveness.

Regarding privately run prisons, the former governor of Tennessee stated,

> If private management is good enough for our sick mothers, it's good enough for our murderers and rapists. (Harms and Allen, 1987, p. 29)

Conversely, Mark Conniff, executive director of the National Association of Criminal Justice, states:

> It's a sad day when a government says we're going to send you to prison but we don't feel competent enough to run the prison so we're going to turn to the private sector and let them administer the punishment. (Harms and Allen, 1987, p. 29)

THE ULTIMATE PUNISHMENT: DEATH

Probably the most difficult of the ethical controversies that exist in corrections is capital punishment. In 2004, 59 inmates were executed and in 2003, 3,415 persons were on death row in the United States (Death Penalty Information Center, 2005)

Currently there are five forms of execution: lethal injection, electrocution, gas, hanging (in two states) and firing squad. Obviously, corrections officials must think that lethal injection is the most humane of the five forms of execution. It is certainly easier on the witnesses and less expensive to administer. In reality, there is no absolute humane form of putting one's fellow man to death, a fact that must have crossed the mind of the families of victims many times.

Some scholars, such as Ernest van den Haag (1986), believe that "executions deter murder," while others think that there is no justification for taking another human life, and that it only deters the condemned. Ethically, there is the possibility of someone innocent being put to death. Since 1900, twenty-five such cases have been documented in the United States (Bureau of Justice Statistics, 1996). To many this is an acceptable risk because the chance of this happening is so small, but one must take into account that when such a mistake occurs it cannot be reversed (Cabana, 1996). What if the innocent person were a family member or even the reader? The documentary *The Thin Blue Line* poignantly follows just such a case, which fortunately resulted in the innocent man's release from prison. Recognizing these risks, in 1997 the American Bar Association (ABA) called for a moratorium on the death penalty, pending safeguards from the states that will guarantee fairness with due process and minimal risk to innocent parties. In January 2003, Illinois Governor George Ryan commuted the sentences of all 164 inmates on death row in Illinois to life in prison without parole and shortened the sentences of 3 others to 40 years. Borrowing the words of the late U.S. Supreme Court Justice Harry Blackmun, Ryan declared, "Because the Illinois death penalty system is arbitrary and capricious—and therefore immoral—I no longer shall tinker with the machinery of death" (Possley and Mills, 2003).

When one takes a life maliciously or commits a heinous crime that calls for the death penalty, the prevailing argument in support is that a conscious and total disregard for society's rules and the life of others warrant society's most severe penalty—death by execution. This powerful argument is countered by an equally strong argument that life is protected by law and that it is inconsistent with the purpose of law to take a life under the guise of the administration of justice, no matter what the crime.

As to trends, the United Nations has listed the death penalty as a human rights violation (United Nations Commission, 1997). The death penalty is now outlawed in England, most of Europe, and most of the English-speaking Western world, except the United States (Amnesty International, 2005). In the United States, thirty-eight states had instituted the death penalty by year-end in 1995 (Bureau of Justice Statistics, 1996), in addition to the federal government. The federal government prescribes execution for over forty offenses, including treason and mailing a bomb with intent to murder. It can be concluded that the international trend is against the death penalty, and the trend in the United States is in the opposite direction.

SUMMARY

Corrections is encompassed with ethical considerations, each one resulting in some degree of controversy and debate. One needs to understand that when someone crosses the line from a free society to a controlled prison or jail environment, the person in question does not give up basic human rights and other ethical considerations. Problems such as violence, health care, overcrowding, correctional officer brutality, and constitutional rights cannot be overlooked just because they occur within the walls of a correctional facility. Yet debate remains concerning to what extent such rights should be administered.

Society often ignores the plight of correctional facilities and feels that such problems do not concern them, but they do—and ethically, society's best interests are served by making sure that corrections is a viable part of society, not a separate entity.

References

American Bar Association. (1997). *Moratorium on the death penalty*, February 3.

American Civil Liberties Union. (1996). *Death penalty*. Available from www.ACLU.org.

Amnesty International. (2005). *The death penalty: Abolitionist and retentionist countries*. Available from www.Amnesty.org.

Argersinger v. Hamlin. (1972). 407 US 25.

Baker v. Holden. (1992). 787 F. Supp. 1008.

Baldasar v. Illinois. (1980). 446 US 222.

Barnes v. Castle. (1977). 561 F. 2nd. 983.

Bell v. Wolfish. (1979). 441 US 520.

Blair-Bey v. Nix. (1992). 113 S.Ct. 620.

Bone v. Commissioner of Prisons. (1994). 1994 WL 383590 (E.D.) 434.

Bounds v. Smith. (1976). 430 US 817.

Bruscino v. Carlson. (1988). 854 F.2nd. 162.

Bureau of Justice Statistics. (2005). Capital punishment statistics. U.S. Dept. of Justice, Office of Justice Programs. Available: http://www.ojp.usdog.gov/bjus/cp.htm

Cabana, D. A. (1996). *Death at midnight*. Boston: Northeastern University Press.

Canedy v. Boardman. (1992). 16 F.3rd. 183.

Coker v. Georgia. (1977). 97 S.Ct. 2861, 433 US 584.

Cole, G. F. (1988). *Criminal Justice: Law and politics*. Belmont, CA: Wadsworth Inc.

Cruz v. Beto. (1971). 405 US 319.

Death Penalty Information Center. (2005). Facts about the death penalty, October 1, 2005. Available: http://deathpenalty.org/FactSheet.pdf

DeMallory v. Cullen. (1988). 855 F.2nd. 442.

Dilulio, J. J., Jr. (1988). What's wrong with private prisons? *The Public Interest*, Summer:92.

Estelle v. Gamble. (1976). 429 US 97.

Fleischer, M. (1989). *Warehousing violence*. Newbury Park, CA: Sage Publications.

Furman v. Georgia. (1972). 408 US 238.

Gates v. Collier. (1971). 616 F.2nd. 1268, 1980.

Gregg v. Georgia. (1976). 428 US 153.

Grummett v. Rushen. (1985). 779 F.2nd 491.

Harms, K. J. and Allen, F. W. (1987). Privatizing prisons. *American City and County*, August:102 (8).

Hernandez v. Estelle. (1986). 788 F.2nd. 1154.

Howard v. Wheaton. (1987). 688 F. Supp. 1140.

Hudson v. Palmer. (1984). 468 US 517.

Hudson v. McMillan. (1992). 503 US 1.

Ingraham, B. L. and Wellford, C. F. (1987). The totality of conditions test in Eighth Amendment litigation. *America's correctional crisis.* Westport, CT: Greenwood Press, Inc.

Johnson v. Avery. (1969). 393 US 483.

Johnson, R. (1987). *Hard times.* Belmont, CA: Brooks Cole Publishing Co.

Langbein, J. H. (1976). The historical origins of the sanction of imprisonment for serious crime. *Journal of Legal Studies*, 5.

Martinson, R. (1974). What works—Questions and answers about prison reform. *The Public Interest,* Spring.

Mary of Oakknoll v. Coughlin. (1985). 101 App Div 2d 931.

Mercer v. Griffin. (1981). 20 Cr.L. 2058.

Michenfelder v. Summer. (1988). 839 F.2nd. 328.

Miller v. Evans. (1992). 832 P.2nd. 786.

Monitor Savings Bank v. Vinson. (1986). 477 US 55.

Mullen, J. (1987). State responses to prison crowding: The politics of change. *America's correctional crisis.* Westport, CT: Greenwood Press Inc.

Newman v. Alabama. (1977). 438 US 781.

Palmer, J. (1997). *Constitutional rights of prisoners*, 5th ed. Cincinnati: Anderson Publishing Co.

Parnell v. Waldrep. (1981). 511 F. Supp. 764.

Pepperling v. Crist. (1984). 739 F2d 443.

Possley, M., and Mills, S. (2003). Clemency for all. *Chicago Tribune*, January 12, pp. 1, 15.

Procunier v. Martinez. (1974). 416 US 396.

Religious Freedom Restoration Act. (1993).

Rhodes v. Chapman. (1981). 452 US 337.

Robinson v. California. (1962). 370 US 660.

Schack v. Wainwright. (1967). 392 US 915.

Sechrest, L., White, S. O., and Brown, E. (1979). *The rehabilitation of criminal offenders: Problems and prospects.* Washington, DC: National Academy of Sciences.

Sheley v. Dugger. (1987). 833 F.2nd. 1420.

Sizemore v. Williford. (1987). 829 F.2nd. 608.

Smith v. Bounds. (1988). 657 F. Supp. 1322.

Sykes, G. M. (1958). *The society of captives: A study of a maximum security prison.* NJ: Princeton University Press.

Taylor v. Sterret. (1976). 532 F2d 462.

Taylor, W. B. (1993). *Brokered justice.* Columbus: Ohio State University Press.

Thornburg v. Abbott. (1989). 490 US 401.

Travis, L., Schwartz, M., and Clear, T. (1983). *Corrections: An issues approach.* Cincinnati, OH: Anderson Publishing Company.

Tribble v. Gardner. (1988). 860 F.2nd. 321.

Turner v. Safeley. (1987). 482 US 78.

U.S. Department of Justice. (1996). Bureau of Justice Statistics. *Capital Punishment.* Washington, DC: Government Printing Office.

U.S. Department of Justice. (1997). Bureau of Justice Statistics. *Prison and jail inmates midyear 1996.* Washington, DC: Government Printing Office.

United Nations, Commission on Human Rights. (1997). Geneva, Switzerland, April 3.

van den Haag, E. (1986). Death and deterrence. *National Review,* March:38.

Vito, G. F. (1983). Reducing the use of imprisonment. *Corrections: An issues approach.* Cincinnati, OH: Anderson Publishing Company.

Walsh v. Brewer. (1980). 450 US 1041.

Walsh v. Mellas. (1988). 837 F2d 789.

Washington v. Harper. (1990). 494 US 210.

Washington v. Lee. (1968). 390 US 333.

Webster's new international dictionary. (1969). Cambridge, MA: Riverside Press.

Whitley v. Albers. (1981). 475 US 321.

Wilkins, L. T. (1969). *Evaluation of penal measures.* New York: Random House.

Wilson v. Seiter. (1991). 489 US 1024.

Young v. Quinlan. (1992). 960 F.2nd. 351.

CASE 1

Anyone Want a Job?

The community college has been a good place to teach, but for the third year in a row there have been no pay raises for faculty and staff. This means that what started out as a decent entry-level teaching position in criminal justice is now a touch-and-go situation. Twenty-eight thousand dollars for a nine-month position, teaching four courses with thirty to forty students each (plus field trips), the Criminal Justice Association, and the thirty-mile commute have taken their toll. Now, with a new baby in the family and a three percent inflation rate each year, things are too tight for comfort. You need another job.

On your last visit to the Southeastern State Correctional Institution with your students, you pointed out a list of jobs posted outside the prison. Your students are interested because this is the list they will be using for a reference when it is their time to apply. You always show your students these lists because anyone can see the monetary value of their college education, i.e., approximately $10.00 an hour with a GED or high school education, $12.00 with a 2-year degree, and $15.00 to start with a four-year degree.

At the bottom of the list you noticed an entry that has been there every time you have pointed out the list to your students—"Training Director, $39–44,000." Although the pay seemed excellent, you had not been interested because you were happy in your current job. However, another year without a pay raise has resulted in you being more than interested. A call to the personnel office at the penitentiary is encouraging; they are very interested. In addition to the usual state requirements of U.S. citizenship, age, and a felony-free record, five years experience in teaching or training, and a master's degree in education or criminal justice, the ability to organize and manage prisoner and staff training programs is also a requirement. One of the hidden advantages not in the advertisement is that there is housing on the prison grounds and all the help one needs with domestic chores, not to mention the pay increase of at least $10,000.

Your resume looks impressive. You have a paragraph to cover each mandatory qualification including your three years as a drill sergeant in the army military police, your two years working in the county jail while in college, and your three years teaching at the community college in which you administered every aspect of the community college educational process for your forty-four criminal justice students. You are also familiar with the surrounding educational institutions from which you graduated and maintain close contact with the faculty, an ideal situation for getting resources for staff development programs. Further, the vocational-technical school director at the community college had, in the past, expressed to you an interest in setting up some pre-release training at the penitentiary if an opportunity to do so ever presented itself.

You were pleased with your application and resume when you submitted them to the state's central personnel office. If the central personnel board finds you qualified, they will put your name on the list and forward it to the Southeastern State Correctional Institution where the vacancy exists, and you could be interviewed in a matter of one or two weeks.

You began to tie up some loose ends at the community college, trying not to be obvious. You hope to be employed elsewhere in the near future, and to renew some old ties at the nearby state university from which you graduated.

Finally, the letter arrived from the State Personnel Office. You were shocked to read that the advertised vacancy had been withdrawn because of "a lack of qualified applicants," but you are invited to reapply if and when the search is reopened. Could it be that the job is being held for someone else?

Your talk with the personnel officer at the correctional facility confirmed your worst fears. There had been plenty of applications, but there was also apparently some infighting in the state capital about the position. The question centered around an internal transfer for the assistant director of the pre-release center—who is strongly supported by the state senator from that district—who just happens to be on the Appropriations Committee. The commissioner seems to think the job is too important to be filled by a person whose only qualifications are those of an assistant manager of a pre-release program. To stop the bickering, the personnel board, an autonomous board appointed by the governor to oversee all the civil service positions in the state, withdrew the advertisement. The position still exists and is currently unfilled, but funding to support it may be moved elsewhere to fill another budgetary need. You want the position so badly you can taste it, but what can you do?

Questions for Discussion

How can you pursue the position? Should you apply for a lesser position at the Southeastern Correctional Institution and then try to transfer into the training director's position? Or should you contact the state senator from your district and ask for his help, risking a premature announcement to the community college that you are looking for another job? Could you file a lawsuit in federal court, claiming that you have not been given an equal opportunity to compete for a state job for which you are qualified, or do you want to continue as you are and hope the job is readvertised? Perhaps there are other options. What will your next move be?

CASE 2

Who's Running the Prison?

You came to the state correctional system with good credentials: an ex-military officer whose fifteen years in high-level correctional management positions and recently completed master's degree in criminal justice make you well qualified for almost any correctional-related position. You have a practical, no-nonsense attitude and feel quite comfortable in your new position as superintendent of the state penitentiary, which had been suffering from incompetent leadership and political intrigue.

The facility is in the state's most isolated corner, and the inmates there either are considered to have little potential for rehabilitation or were serving such long-term sentences that rehabilitation was of little immediate interest. In accepting the job as superintendent, you stated that your top priorities were to upgrade conditions in the prison, especially the physical plant, and to improve the quality of the correctional officer staff. Recently the two problems have become entwined in an unexpected way.

You had only been on the job for one week when the county commissioner for the district in which your institution is located came to see you. The commissioner, as you soon learned, was a political power in the county and could make conditions miserable for you if he wanted to. It seems that his son-in-law needed a job and he wanted you to find a place for him on your staff. One word led to another, and before you knew it you responded by stating, "Hell no! I won't hire anybody unless they are qualified." The county commissioner left angrily, and a day later Senator Nester called. Senator Nester was on the state corrections committee and represented the district in which your institution was located. At the time he called you, you did not know that he was also on the appropriations committee. You learned later that if someone wanted a management job at the institution, he had to call Senator Nester in order to be hired.

Senator Nester stated in his call to you that he just wanted to "get acquainted" and give you a little friendly advice. First, he indicated that you should make a serious effort to get along with all the local officials, and second, he recommended that you hire the county commissioner's son-in-law. You told the senator that you would look at the son-in-law's application when he submitted it, and if he was qualified, you would give him serious consideration, but beyond that you could make no promises.

Your review of the son-in-law's hastily submitted application revealed that he had a high school diploma, had been a police officer on a local force, and had held several other unrelated jobs—all of rather short duration. In short, he might be qualified for an entry-level correctional officer slot. However, his work record was spotty and the reason for his departure from the police department was unclear. Although no one was talking openly about it, there were some allegations of police brutality involving the son-in-law circulating among certain members of the department. Since you did not want an unqualified and questionable political hack in your organization, you placed his application in "file 13."

After a week Senator Nester's office called "on behalf of a constituent" and inquired about the son-in-law's application. Your personnel officer told the senator's office that a letter had been sent to the applicant thanking him for his application, but informing him that applications were competitive and, unfortunately, he had not been selected.

Later in the day Senator Nester called back in person; he was enraged. "Why wasn't I informed of the turn down? I've done a hell of a lot for this correctional system and have a right to expect the courtesy of a reply. I never had this problem before." Nester was clearly threatening when he said, "You may find that these upcoming hearings will question your practices in dealing with the legislature, and I'll have some questions about your personnel policies, too." You finally told Senator Nester that you were running the institution, and until you were replaced you would continue to hire people based on merit.

Two months later at budget hearings in the legislature, you found out Senator Nester was a man of his word. Because of his influence, a new car for the prison superintendent was stricken, slots for eighteen new correctional officers were also stricken, and to make matters worse, the committee voted to nullify the badly needed pay raises that had been budgeted for all the prison employees.

The senator's message has come through to you "loud and clear." You realize that the two of you will have to reach some sort of working agreement, unless you can marshal enough support from other more friendly legislators, which at present does not seem likely.

The question for you now is: how should you approach Senator Nester? How can you maintain your standards and at the same time appease him? Should you give and take a little, should you look for a new job, or should you do both? You are not a quitter; you would prefer to work with Senator Nester, but you keep asking yourself how.

Questions for Discussion

In this particular case, it appears that you, the superintendent, must initiate a reconciliation with the senator. Was the rift that developed between the two of you completely necessary? If you had done your "homework" and had known how powerful the senator was, might you have handled the situation more discreetly? What could you have done differently, and what can you do now?

CASE 3

Offender Rights and Public Expectations

You have been superintendent of the state prison for five years. Having to house, feed, and provide recreation and treatment for 2,000 inmates in a prison built for 1,200 has not made your life exactly easy. In fact, you have recently noticed that you have begun to eat Rolaids like M&Ms. With the correctional officer's union threatening to strike, a stack of inmate lawsuits on your desk, and the typical problems of contraband and cell block assaults, all you need is another problem. Yet here it is. You glance once more at the letter from Reverend Hawkins:

Dear Superintendent Heskins:

As a Christian brother, I entreat you to ban the subversive book circulating among the inmates by the self-proclaimed spiritual teacher who goes by the name of Yogi Bo. His book clearly encourages rebellion against the authority of the State and of God. Our chaplains have a difficult enough time reforming the unfortunate who find themselves in prison with the help of the Good Book. As difficult as it is, they are doing a remarkable job. To allow a book of other writings which challenge the God-given principles our country was founded on to circulate among the inmates will create an overwhelming burden to them and other God-fearing counselors, not to mention the risk of insurrection it poses to prison security.

The Ministerial Association is unanimously recommending that you ban this objectionable book.

We are praying that you will make the proper decision.

Sincerely,
Reverend Hawkins
President of the Ministerial Association

You shake your head, partly in frustration and partly in amusement, and take a deep breath. You were raised as a child in a Protestant church and you and your wife have raised your children likewise. You share most of Reverend Hawkins's beliefs, but regardless of what you and the reverend believe, a great number of inmates don't feel or think the same way. Your prison is made up of Protestant Christians, Catholics, Native Americans, Black Muslims, two Hindus, one Buddhist, and a number of people who, if they believe in anything at all, probably believe in violence.

On the one hand, you have Reverend Hawkins and his supporters who want you to ban Yogi Bo's book. On the other hand, you have a relatively small yet vocal group of inmates who follow the teachings of Yogi Bo. You have read the book, and while you personally disagree with some of its ideas from your Christian viewpoint, you have found nothing advocating violence or rebellion. In fact, its message is basically a positive one and, to your surprise, you find yourself agreeing with a lot of the points Yogi Bo makes.

Popping another Rolaids in your mouth, you know you have got to make a decision. The easy thing to do would be to ban the book. Since the prison is located in a small rural area where Reverend Hawkins has substantial influence, such a decision would be good for you and the prison's image. If you don't ban the book, you will be criticized, letters will be written, and you might not even be reelected elder in the church you and your family attend. Still, you really don't like being pressured from the Ministerial Association, and the book isn't the threat that Reverend Hawkins and others think it is. In fact, you wonder if they have even read it. You reach for another Rolaids.

Questions for Discussion

Religious beliefs are very personal and powerful. There will be trouble, no matter which way you decide. What are some issues at stake here regarding the inmates' wishes and rights and the community's expectations? What role should your conscience play in your decision?

A Choice of Punishments

You are an eighteen-year-old high school senior with nothing to do during the summer. No job, no summer school, no camps, nothing. For some reason, public summer programs for youth like you are very scarce or nonexistent. It is July 4th, hot, and you are looking for some diversion. Your friend, Paul Johnson, comes by in his antique pick-up truck that he has spent the last six months rebuilding, and he invites you to a party that he will be attending at a friend's apartment in the projects. The friend's parents are away for the day. Although Paul is a few months older than you and dropped out of your high school, he always seems to have money, not much, but some. Paul tells you that he has to go by the grocery store and pick up a case of beer and also get some gas. You are impressed until Paul drives up to a two-pump Quick Stop, parks beside a car that is filling up so he cannot be seen by the cashier, fills up, then jumps in the truck and drives off. The attendant made the mistake of letting the pump run without being able to see the vehicle being filled up. You are not too happy with this, but it was so slick, the way he edged up to the pumps behind the other automobile, that there seems to be little danger of getting caught.

Next, Paul drives to a grocery store for beer; he parks at the corner of the building out of sight of the cashiers in the store and asks you to watch the truck because he wants to leave the motor running. "Sometimes it is hard to start when it is hot," explains Paul. You patiently wait and in a few minutes Paul comes out the doors of the grocery with a case of beer and drives off. Apparently, Paul legitimately purchased a case of beer and you are going to be able to share it with him at the party. "Good friend, old Paul," you mutter to yourself.

The next day your mother tells you there is a police officer at the door with a warrant for your arrest. Not only did the Quick Stop clerk get a description and partial license plate number, but the manager of the grocery store followed Paul out and got the full tag number as well as a description of the occupants of the truck. Paul has already been arrested and identified you as his companion. In your state, accessories to misdemeanors are treated as principals and you are one. You tell the police officers you were only a passenger. Yes, you helped drink the beer. All right, you rode in a truck with gas you knew was stolen, and you sat in the car when Paul left it running to go get the beer—which Paul apparently stole—but you did not do anything. After your conversation with the investigating officers, you are taken to the police station and booked for two counts of petty larceny, and released to your mother's custody. You are to appear in city court to answer to the charges a week from Monday at 9 AM.

You finally talk to Paul, who apologizes for implicating you but says, "I had no choice." Paul suggests that you and he leave the state since the police will not come after you in another state just for a misdemeanor. You think about it, but you are in enough trouble as it is, and running away would not help anything. You were into some vandalism once before and a couple of incidents of shoplifting and nothing happened other than you had to make restitution, so you decide to go to court and take your chances.

Judge Ward, the city judge, has recently been elected to his post. He is a retired FBI agent who ran on a platform of "getting tough on crime." Judge Ward has been said to not have allowed the phrase *not guilty* to pass his lips since elected. Hard, fair, incorruptible, and knowledgeable, Judge Ward is about to introduce you to a new experience. "I find you guilty," thundered Judge Ward. This was the worst day of your life. The judge said he would defer sentencing until he received a report from the case worker. In the meantime, the case worker would interview you, your family, and some friends before making a recommendation to the judge. You could be looking at six months in jail, a $500 fine, restitution, community service, and maybe more. You cannot believe all this happened to you because you hooked up with Paul on the 4th of July.

You decide to visit the public defender's office for help. Although public defenders in your state are required only to deal with felony cases, maybe you can get some advice. A legal intern in the public defender's office tells you honesty is the best policy, and to cooperate with the case worker. You find out that the case worker functions also as a probation officer. You do not trust this intern's advice. "Say nothing; it is your constitutional right," says Paul.

After an uncooperative interview, you received a summons to Judge Ward's chambers. The case worker will be there, too.

The case worker's report is thorough. It touches on your past arrests, your uncooperativeness, and your denial of guilt. Judge Ward has a number of options: the fine, jail time, restitution probation, public service, or a new military-style training program designed to motivate and teach young offenders respect for authority. This is a federally sponsored program located on a nearby national guard base. What would you do if you were Judge Ward?

Questions for Discussion

A "short, sharp shock" may sometimes be an effective deterrent, but is incarceration for minor offenses a cost-effective method of punishment from either an economic or a social point of view? What corrective measures are most likely to instill a sense of responsibility in this youthful offender? You have read the options. What do you think is the most effective way to adjudicate this case and why? What would you hope for if you were the eighteen-year-old? If you were the eighteen-year-old's parents?

CASE 5

Sexual Harassment

What a mess! You let out a deep sigh as you hang up the telephone. Sitting at your desk, staring out the window, you listen to the rain and slowly try to collect your thoughts.

Janie Smith has just called you in tears. Three years ago she was part of your caseload. This time around she is assigned to Ned, your office supervisor. When Janie was originally assigned to you for case supervision, she had been convicted of drug possession and prostitution. You remember her well: an attractive sixteen-year-old black girl with a one-year-old daughter, a drug addition, a police record, and very little education. You worked with her for two years and watched her gradually dig her way out of the hole she had found herself in, into a life with some hope. She earned a GED degree and with the help and support of a caring grandmother, she learned how to become a mother herself. When she finished her term of probation, she found a job in an upscale department store selling cosmetics and women's fashions. You felt her chances to make it were excellent. She seemed to have improved her sense of self-esteem and had dreams of one day owning and operating her own fashion boutique. Apparently something happened in the year following her release from probation. Who knows? Relapses happen. You have been in the business for fifteen years and it still disappoints you when someone doesn't make it. What makes Janie's current situation even more frustrating is that it involves Ned, your supervisor.

Ned is white, forty-six years old, and divorced. Janie has just tearfully informed you that Ned has grown increasingly aggressive over the last three months in trying to force her into a sexual relationship with him. Apparently he is offering her unsupervised probation in exchange for sexual favors and threatening her with revocation if she refuses his advances. You recall Janie's words, "He told me that since

I was a prostitute, it shouldn't be a big deal. He even offered me money if I was good enough."

You get a sick feeling in your stomach when you recall what she said. You have heard rumors about Ned. This probably isn't the first time he has done something like this. You have never seen any proof of the rumors, so you never accepted them as being true. Besides, Ned has always been good to you. Now you find yourself feeling angry and foolish. This time you are going to have to act. You gave Janie all the reassurance you could and promised to get back to her. You have to respond to this problem, but how? You consider calling Carl Baxter, the regional supervisor, but are uncertain since he and Ned are good friends. In fact, they play golf together every week. You also realize that getting caught in the middle of this problem can harm your own career. After all, you do have a wife and children. Besides, Janie hasn't exactly been a model of virtue. She has brought a lot of this trouble on herself. Still, it isn't right for Ned to abuse his power over a client the way he has. He's white, she's black and a woman, and you are stuck right in the middle of a touchy situation.

Questions for Discussion

How could sexism and racism be a part of Ned's harassment of Janie? Can you think of other potential problems in such settings involving racism and sexism? What about your responsibility as the probation officer caught in the middle? What could be the consequences of your taking action against Ned? Would it be better if you checked out the previous allegations against Ned? What are some safeguards that could be implemented that might deter such harassment as is found in this case?

CASE 6

Outsourcing for Profit

The Department of Corrections decided several years ago to contract out to a private vendor for inmate medical services. As superintendent of a large institution, you have had more than a few occasions to cast a critical eye toward the medical care being provided by the contractor.

You receive a phone call early Saturday morning from the distressed wife of an inmate. Another inmate had called to tell her that at 6 AM her husband had been taken to the prison hospital suffering from what appeared to be a stroke. You calmed the inmate's wife down and assured her you would check on her husband.

Arriving at the hospital at 8:15, you found the inmate in an examination room, unattended. He was unable to converse very well as his speech was slurred. The left side of his face was drooping, and he indicated he could not move his left arm.

You found a nurse and inquired about the inmate's condition. She said he had "probably suffered a stroke but they wouldn't know for sure until the doctor examined him." You looked at your watch and asked if, in fact, the inmate had been waiting two hours and still had not seen a doctor. The nurse replied that on Saturdays the doctor usually came in late unless there was an emergency!

Angrily, you called the company's regional director at home and explained the situation. The regional director responded that if you wanted a physician on duty on weekends, it would cost the department additional money.

Questions for Discussion

How can this issue be addressed when the medical care does not fall within our sphere of authority? How can increasing efficiency regarding financial savings for the corrections department result in increased human costs? What is a proper balance between maintaining fiscal responsibility and inmate health care?

The Public Has a Right to Know

Overcrowding in correctional institutions at the state level has come to be a fact of life in most states. It is a consequence of many things, including tougher sentencing and parole laws, reduction in the age of criminal culpability for juveniles, and lagging community programs. Your state is no exception. As director of classification, you have tried every device you can think of to sub-classify your inmates into groups according to their needs and the institution's require-ment to provide a safe and healthy environment in which rehabilita-tion can be practiced, and in which control, in the sense of security, can be maintained. Someone started the job long ago when they designated your facility a medium-security institution, but with the population now at almost 40% over the original design capacity, and with the central office daily dumping more and more inmates into your office, the process of providing basic housing outweighs an acute need for selective assignment and treatment.

You have kept the warden fully aware of the classification prob-lem; that space considerations were dictating the rules of classifica-tion, and particularly the crisis in the hospital unit. Not only are the geriatric inmates becoming a larger part of your population, they also require more medical care with problems like renal failure, liver dis-ease, cancer and heart disease. However, the huge influx of HIV-pos-itive inmates, products of dirty needles and unprotected sex, are actually prompting you to put many chronically ill inmates into the general population, unless their symptoms are so severe that they cannot work and require ongoing care by medical personnel. Actu-ally, some new drugs seem to be helping with the pain and suffering of some diseases, but that does not solve the problem that you have now: what to do with the growing number of prisoners who require special medical attention. At any rate, you had just as soon not meet with Bob Short of the *Times Herald*. He has been assigned to write a series of articles on prison costs in response to some letters to the editor on the skyrocketing costs of medical services as reflected in the department of corrections budget just submitted to the legislature. The corrections budget now exceeds the budget for the community colleges. People do not seem to realize that persons incarcerated by the state have a right to safety and basic medical care just as much as people in the free world.

It is two o'clock and time for Mr. Short's arrival. You wish you had all the answers, and most of all, you wish the warden had handled this instead of you!

Bob Short's questions are what you would expect from a seasoned investigative journalist—well thought out, concise, and aimed directly at the heart of the problem. "How many persons are incarcerated here?" Short asks.

"Twenty-nine hundred and fifty-six," you respond, "depending on how many we gained or lost since 6 AM this morning." You want Short to know you are right on top of the problem.

"How many persons was this prison built to house?" Short continued.

"The original plans called for 2,000 beds, additional building has upped capacity to 2,300," you respond. You continue, "That may not seem like much, only 600 over, about 28%, and they all have bunks, but the programs are all messed up. We cannot do much 'correcting'; I'd like to know who coined that word, and certainly our rehabilitative and social programs are overwhelmed to the point of being ineffective. Overcrowding adversely affects everything—the staff, the inmates, all of their families—everything. But cope we must, and cope we will."

Short takes notes and remarks, "I think most people understand that prison overcrowding is a problem, but they do not understand the associated costs that come with it, like the program breakdowns and something you did not mention, medical costs." Short looked directly in your eyes—this is what he is after. "Let me ask you this," Short continues, "How many persons do you have here who are HIV positive, or do you test them?"

You respond, "About 10%; this morning there were six new cases diagnosed and reported. From diagnosis to release or death, as the case may be, our inmates are here for an average of eight years. We figure we spend $18,000 per year on drugs and treatment for those with HIV. This is above the normal cost of incarceration."

"What is the normal cost?" Short probes.

You reply, "Hard to figure exactly because there are capital, brick and mortar costs, socioeconomic costs such as loss of income and income turn-around, family depending on public support, etc. But for an idea of the costs, you can take the population incarcerated and divide that into the annual appropriation, less capital improvements. That would be about $11,000 per inmate. That includes food, guard salaries, and so on, but it does not tell the whole story. It is just a number."

Short looks at you questioningly and comments, "Social costs are always hard to figure. They are full of counterbalancing variables— for example, if you did not have any prisoners, all the guards would be out of work. But let me get to the meat of this subject," Short continues. "Your sick people, persons dying with cancer, the HIV group, your geriatric inmates, what do you do with them?"

"I wish you had not asked," you say. "Basically, they are in with the general population if they can manage. We do not have the room to set up special care programs for them. They will stay in the population until they cannot take care of their own needs, then they will go to the hospital and die. A few will be released before they die due to expiration of sentence. I wish we could do better, but with current inmate population trends, it looks like there is no end to the problem."

Short folds his notebook and says, "How about the governor— could he not release some of your sickest prisoners?"

"He could," you reply, "under his executive clemency powers he can commute, pardon, and reprieve, but he will not. He wants the scales of justice to apply equally to all regardless of age, health, or wealth."

Short prepares to leave the room, "I will not quote you because I know you cannot criticize the governor, but what would you do?"

You ponder Short's questions for the rest of your shift. What *would* you do, if you had the power?

Questions for Discussion

Conditions caused by prison overcrowding account for many of the lawsuits and other problems confronting prison administrators. The irony is that the cost to repair the deficit conditions may be less than the cost of defense of the lawsuits and the human costs arising from the years of neglect suffered by the corrections systems. How would you approach the problem of the sick, the elderly, and particularly the HIV infected inmates? Consider integration, isolation, and early release as long term measures. What would you do short term for expediency?

CASE 8

Watch What You Say

As commissioner of corrections you are frequently invited to address various civic groups and other organizations. You enjoy these occasions for the most part. They are good public forums in which to discuss the goals of the department and brag on its successes. Recently, you addressed a noontime civic club meeting. Although you had not been aware that any members of the press were in attendance, it would not have mattered if you had known. You did not say anything that, in your opinion, was especially controversial. During a brief question-and-answer session at the end of your speech, you were asked to talk for a moment about the state's spiraling prison population, which had doubled in the last eight years. Your response included a comment that the legislature needed to maximize the use of other less expensive options, rather than relying on incarceration so much.

The next day, the local newspaper ran a somewhat dramatic editorial in support of your comments. That afternoon you received a phone call from an extremely irate Lester Knowles, chairman of the Senate Committee on Penitentiaries. He reminded you in no uncertain terms that your job was to enforce policies, not make them. Later that day, another senator, Sue Atkins, who is head of a task force on correctional reform, also contacted you to request that you advise her and her blue-ribbon panel on the topic of correctional alternatives. Since you were a former probation officer at the start of your career, you have been on both sides of the fence. While you are confident that you could offer substantial insight to Senator Atkins' task force, you know you would be doing so at your own peril: you also realize that Senator Knowles would definitely not approve.

Questions for Discussion

Prison overcrowding may or may not be a problem for Senator Knowles or the governor, but it is a real and pressing problem in your world. How do you respond to two senators who have conflicting interests and priorities? What is the right course of action for you to take?

The Correctional Administrator

The effective correctional administrator, whether in a community or a more traditional institutional setting, must be a person who possesses significant management and interpersonal skills.

The seven cases and text in this section will provide you with a sampling of what problems you might expect as a correctional administrator. Being a female superintendent of a women's prison, dealing with political pressures from within and without the correctional agency, and attempting to solve the problems of prison sexuality are some of the difficult situations you will be given to react to in this section.

INTRODUCTION

In the 1960s and 1970s, correctional administrators became more dependent upon the treatment staff for providing meaningful rehabilitative efforts for inmates. The question of the "right to treatment" emerged from this change in emphasis. The term "right to treatment" was first used in an American Bar Association publication stressing the fact that society recognized criminals possessed a moral right to treatment. However, at that time, they had established no legal right to treatment (Birnhaum, 1960). During the past several decades, American courts were inundated with cases from correctional institutions addressing this issue. The goals of correctional administration were altered because of this litigation. Correctional institutions gradually moved from a primary perspective of custody and punishment to that of treatment. Although the pendulum has swung back toward custody and punishment, treatment has remained a vital issue regarding the adjustment and maintenance of inmates in correctional environments (Irwin and Austin, 1997).

The development of new philosophies of custody in correctional institutions (and the emerging rights of inmates to treatment) served to emphasize treatment possibilities correctional administrators should provide. New priorities slowly entered the correctional scheme of policy and operation. Many correctional administrators now believe that punishing offenders is the role of the judicial system, not the correctional system (Marshall, 1981; Innes, 1997). An implicit aspect of custody is treatment as well as the explicit function of fulfilling society's legal expectations.

Correctional administrators face a series of challenging tasks in the development of both treatment and custody goals for corrections. Because of the role of their position, correctional administrators are often faced with problems that inhibit their responsibilities and potential new developments. Among these problems are social and political influences and correctional traditions and fragmentation of the correctional process.

In addition, the organization of the correctional institution can lead to a fragmentation of services and responsibilities within the institution itself. The administrator must serve two basic interest groups: employees within the organization (treatment staff and custodial staff) as well as the inmate population. Figure 1 depicts a typical organizational chart of a maximum-security prison facility.

Figure 1 Maximum Security Prison Organization Chart

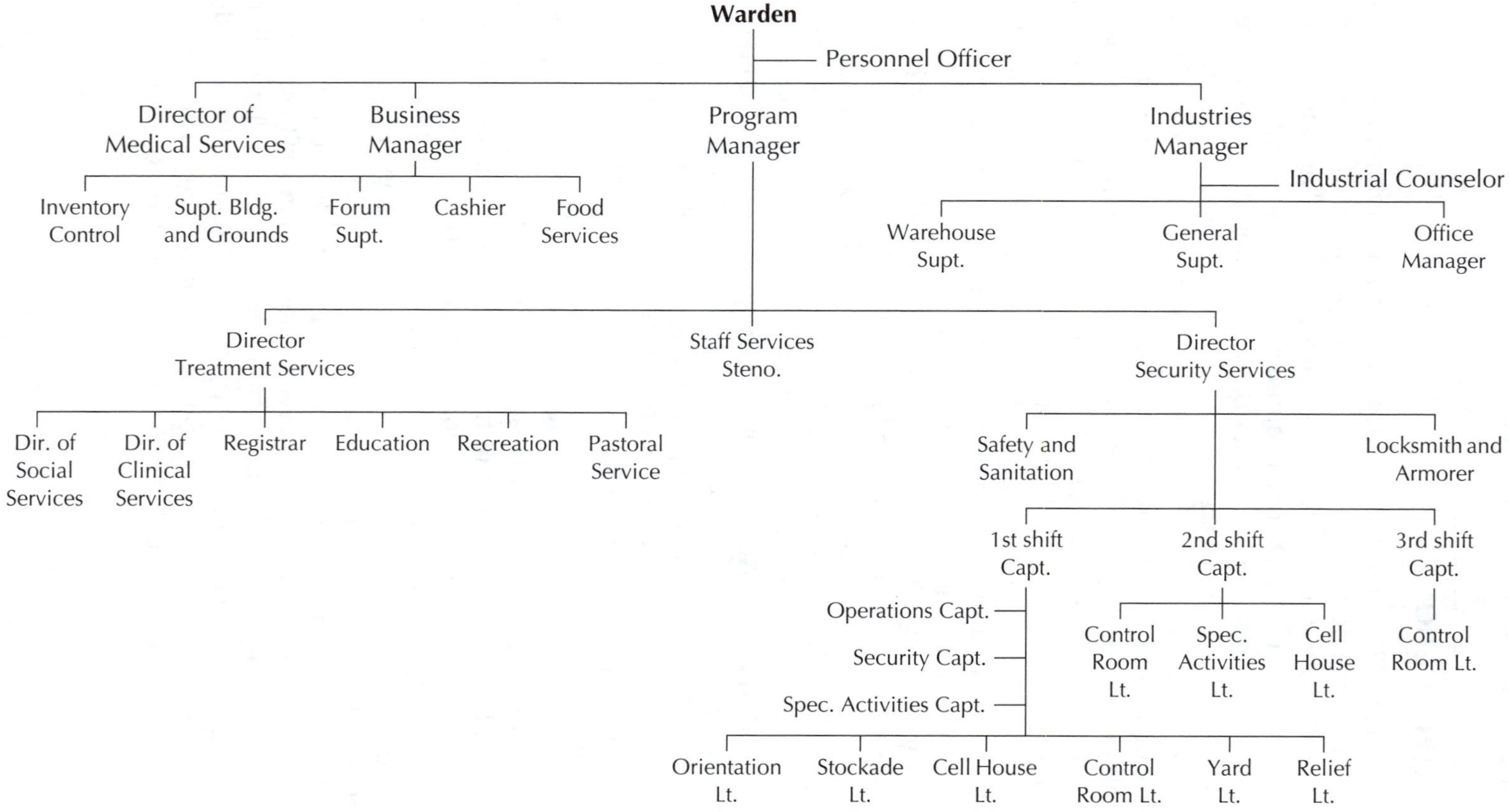

SOCIAL AND POLITICAL INFLUENCES

There are a number of social and political influences in the correctional setting including: (1) a spoils system, (2) a weak civil service system, (3) economic issues, and (4) public attitudes (Irwin, 1980). Correctional administrators need to recognize these influences and learn to deal with them if their goals are to be realized.

In effect, a political spoils system operates in many branches of government. Higher-level administrators often change with the shifts of political power. In most states, correctional commissioners are appointed by the governor. With each new commissioner, ripples of power shifts reverberate throughout the administrative structure. When changes are initiated in the upper quadrant of correctional administration, the impact can even be felt by recently sentenced offenders.

The civil service process is designed to balance these shifts in top administration by allowing qualified employees in middle management positions and line workers to remain in their positions. This process is, however, weak enough to be overridden by those persons who possess substantial political power, particularly at state levels. Lawmakers may be inclined to reject a strong civil service system which is receptive to their party's control Subsequently, even with state protection laws, a department head can reorganize a division with relative ease, including the deletion of previous administrators. Such practices can weaken the correctional system and facilitate changes in administrative policies frequently enough to render it largely ineffective.

Correctional administrators must be good salespersons, possess good public-relations characteristics, and must promote the importance of a large maintenance and treatment budget to superiors, legislators, and the public (Thomas and Hepburn, 1983). Treatment for offenders is expensive because it requires well-trained, qualified personnel. Effective correctional treatment often requires meaningful programs, additional staff, and equipment. Legislators are inclined to favor more short-term, cost-effective efforts. However, specific treatment programs may require long-term measurement to determine effectiveness. It is often difficult for politically minded legislators and governors to make expensive commitments to correctional treatment when custodial care is much more economical for short-term measurement, not to mention pro-punishment public opinion.

Many governors and legislators use the ideals in corrections to constitute superficial improvements in the system that are, for the most part, ineffective. Many nineteenth-century prisons have been demolished and replaced with smaller "community corrections" facilities in the name of social change and correctional reform. A large, central prison is replaced with five to ten smaller local institutions with new staff and custodial personnel. In such instances, treatment can remain just as ineffective as with the central prison, but with millions of tax dollars spent for a "face lift."

Social attitudes play an important role in the effectiveness of correctional programs. Every few decades, the pendulum of social attitudes seem to sway from one extreme to the other. Generally, these social attitudes are governed largely by economic values. During times of economic growth, public attitudes tend to support social treatment and services. When the economy is poor, public attitudes tend to reflect more conservative beliefs. During the 1960s, many entitlement programs and social services were made available based on public demands and concerns (e.g., social welfare, poverty, social security, medicare–medicaid, health and safety programs, etc.). During that time of economic stability, social legislation became abundant and many law enforcement and corrections court decisions were instituted favoring "rights" of the accused and incarcerated; reflecting the social attitudes of the time. As the economy deteriorated in the late 1970s, public attitudes became more conservative, increasingly favoring punishment and deterrence over the treatment of offenders. In the 1980s and 1990s a rise in media attention to crime issues may have also fueled the public's desire for more punitive sanctions toward offenders. Televised court proceedings, police documentaries, and "most wanted" shows coupled with the public's frustration with the criminal justice system seem to have created public demands for harsher penalties (Kappeler and Potter, 2005; Innes, 1997).

CORRECTIONAL TRADITIONS AND FRAGMENTATION

Social institutions often embody traditions that lend strength and stability during times of change. However, this inherent element can also inhibit their ability to change. Of all government institutions, corrections may be most bound by tradition. A good example is the litigation that has challenged correctional administrators over the past couple of decades. Administrators who have chosen to ignore prisoners' rising awareness of their rights have been deluged with lawsuits.

Dedicated correctional personnel who have spent many years in correctional institutions are concerned for their own jobs and safety as well as those of society. Every government agency has a core of administrative staff who, through a sense of motivation and loyalty, remain on the job even when monetary rewards fall well below the normal scale. For such individuals, the desire to serve is fulfilled by their roles. To succeed in such an environment, many employees often model themselves after those persons who have recently moved up the promotional ladder. Such practices are typically non-threatening to supervisors and strengthen tradition within corrections. Employees who are promoted through this process can become "institutionalized" within the bureaucracy. While they may not implement correctional policies, they do administer them. Since they were promoted by a "status quo" model, tradition under their supervision can to a large extent control the destiny of corrections in a similar fashion. Consequently, change in correctional processes may occur more easily on paper than in a literal sense.

Effective correctional administration should work toward overcoming the fragmented nature of the correctional process. Few lawmakers realize that offenders need a continuous treatment program in order to move from the judicial process back into society as well as adjust to the different correctional environments in which they must exist. Probation is controlled by one system of corrections, parole another, juveniles another, and so on. Correctional administrators need to realize that they can control only a small portion of the entire treatment program for offenders. According to the National Advisory Commission on Criminal Justice Standards and Goals (1973), offenders are handled by city, county, and state agencies within the correctional system with different policies and views on treatment held by each.

The fragmentation in corrections may be fueled by the emergence of community corrections programs. Using the same time-worn standards of control on funding and policy at local, state and federal levels, community corrections often exhibits characteristics as disorganized as the old centralized prison institutions. An assortment of health, welfare and youth responsibilities converge within corrections, although their primary function is typically not corrections. Public disenchantment with prisons as a solution to the rehabilitation and reintegration of offenders, including the general movement toward the community-based corrections concept, can serve to increase the divisiveness within corrections. In this sense, all problems in the correctional arena are not self-induced.

CORRECTIONAL MANAGEMENT

In 1960, Myrl Alexander, who later became director of the Federal Bureau of Prisons, addressed a gathering of criminal justice professionals on changes that corrections could anticipate during the coming decades. Alexander (1960) stated, "the best management practice is one which integrates the total activities and services toward the goal of curing criminality." Alexander's prophecies have had much impact on the methods and ideologies of correctional treatment. Correctional treatment and rehabilitation is based on the premise that criminality can be treated or "cured." There are many sociological and psychological theories for correctional treatment, most of which have been applied in one manner or another in corrections (e.g., individual therapy, group therapy, counseling, social work, psychological measurement, etc.). However, serious questions have been raised about the effectiveness of correctional treatment and rehabilitation and many experts are advocating a more punitive approach to dealing with law violators (Martinson, 1980).

Correctional treatment consists of two basic components: (1) institutional treatment, and (2) community-based treatment. Personnel employed in institutional treatment programs include prison guards, professional treatment staff, administrators, and support staff. While it is the primary responsibility of professional treatment staff to "diagnose" and "treat" offenders, treatment, administrative and management personnel should be participatory. In other words, the entire personnel should be involved in the integration of treatment and rehabilitative efforts to inmates. The failure of administrators, prison guards and custodial staff to support treatment programs could be a contributing factor to the recidivism rates of institutional corrections. Feldman (1972) found the lowest success rates of rehabilitation programs in closed correctional institutions. Community-based correctional treatment programs seem to have shown more success regarding rehabilitation efforts. This appears due, in part, to the environmental conditions found in closed institutions and the failure of an integrated treatment program involving all members of the correctional personnel.

If any measurable success in offender rehabilitation is to be found in closed correctional facilities, the line workers (e.g., prison guards and staff) and administrators will have to be adequately trained in and practice, therapeutic methods as an integrated whole. Given the physical and social structure of a prison facility, one will find many of the same crisis problems found "on the outside." Racial conflicts, potential riots, sexual assaults, violence, suicide, divorce, and death of family members are all crisis problems found in prisons as frequently as they are "on the outside" (Bowker, 1983). Police officers have found that training in crisis intervention skills helps prevent more serious conflicts from erupting (Roberts, 1976). The same skills are required of prison guards and administrators in what is often a more potentially explosive environment.

Correctional administrators should not rely entirely on treatment personnel to handle therapy with inmates. Policies and procedures developed by administrators should follow an integrated treatment approach, including training of line workers in crisis intervention and counseling techniques. Too many correctional institutions seem split between administrative and line workers who lean more towards punishment methods and the counseling personnel who lean more towards treatment methods. With proper correctional management, many serious conflicts and incidents of violence may be prevented in closed correctional institutions.

All too often, correctional administrators find themselves involved in "management by crisis." In other words, such administrators solve each problem as it arises without taking into consideration the long-range implications of the solutions and without seeking means by which the problem can be permanently eliminated. The administrator has a number of means available which he/she can use to monitor and control the prison operation. These include reports, records, and frequent evaluations. For example, an increase in the number of disciplinary reports may indicate to an alert administrator, an escalation in prisoner dissatisfaction. The administrator's evaluation of the situation may point to poor menu planning, poor supervisory procedures, or to some new and unpopular administrative procedure. If such a problem is recognized and analyzed, it is possible to seek solutions to the situation before it becomes a serious problem.

A major crisis facing correctional facility administrators is the control of infectious diseases. The rapid increase in cases of Acquired Immunodeficiency Syndrome (AIDS) has caused fear and uncertainty among correctional administrators and employees. Issues such as education, screening, precautionary measures, costs of services and medical care, and legal issues dealing with equal rights are major problems for correctional facilities (Quinn, 2003; Whitehead et al., 2004). Since homosexuality and intravenous drug use are major causes for the spread of the disease, the impact to correctional facilities could be significant (Hammett, 1989).

Our social values and correctional theories have been ambivalent about what should be done with, to, and for criminals. Consequently, it is not surprising to find that correctional work has been characterized by ambivalent values, conflicting goals and norms, and contradictory ideologies. Cressey (1968) indicates that "such a state of flux is not necessarily an impediment to correctional innovation." Given such a state of ambivalence, correctional administrators may experiment with a variety of innovative methods of management and treatment without exceeding the boundaries of acceptable correctional administration. Correctional organizations are typically structured to resist change and any "experimentation" in innovation must be done slowly with discretion and keeping various interest groups in mind (e.g., prison guards, treatment staff, political influences, social values, etc.).

Glaser (1971) has suggested five methods for research that correctional administrators may use to improve correctional services: (1) procure the most complete post-release information obtainable on offenders; (2) focus presentation of post-release data on the responsibilities the correctional agency must meet, especially on cost-effectiveness; (3) attempt to determine the economic problems of inmate releases; (4) correctional administration and research should try to comprehend the total circumstances of an offender's current situation and his view of these circumstances; and (5) correctional improvement proposals will be most readily supported if they are introduced piecemeal and include procedures for measuring effectiveness. Glaser (1971) maintains that by following these suggestions, administrators will promote correctional research with the data compilation and can justify their financial requests for necessary funds with more adequacy.

PRIVATE CORRECTIONS

The privatization of corrections has become popular in a number of states in recent years. By 1987, three states (Florida, Kentucky and Tennessee) had enacted laws authorizing state contracts to privately operated correctional facilities. A decade later, every state in the union had some privatization of correctional facilities and services. The overcrowding of prisons as well as the cost of construction and operation had led to government contracts with private companies to operate some facilities. Private correctional companies indicate that they can finance and operate prisons at lower costs and still make a profit. Every state currently contracts with private corrections companies to operate some form of correctional service or program.

Proponents of privatization of corrections maintain that it can save government expenditures for corrections, promote competition and provide technical and managerial innovations in the correctional field (Quinn, 2003; Schwartz and Travis, 1997). Opponents of privatization claim that the reduction of operating costs are at the expense of humane treatment and correctional rehabilitative treatment programs. Because of the competitive and profit-making nature of private prisons, management will more likely hire substandard employees and provide substandard correctional treatment programs (Quinn, 2003; Schwartz and Travis, 1997).

SUMMARY

Correctional administrators have found in the last few decades that punishment and treatment inevitably must be balanced with current social values and attitudes. Administrators must be able to cope with social and political influences on correctional ideologies and recognize that the correctional process is fragmented with only a small part of the process under their control.

Because correctional ideologies are ambivalent about recidivism, correctional administrators tend to reflect their own values and attitudes toward rehabilitation and tend to adhere to traditional methods of correctional administration. Administrators have found they are answerable to legislators, the public, and the courts in the methods of rehabilitation and administration used in their respective institutions. Administrators should formulate policies and procedures which not only serve to treat or rehabilitate offenders but also protect public interests and safety. As in any bureaucratic system, correctional administrators must cope with sacrifices in order to obtain gains for their organization.

Running a correctional institution is not an easy task, and the job is becoming harder all the time. Never has the correctional institution—and its administrator—been so visible to the public eye. And never has the correctional institution contained as many paradoxes and problems as it does today. The correctional administrator must continually struggle with the problems of conflicting priorities, limited funds, deficient facilities, and a limited staff. At the same time, the administrator is expected to find ways to develop his/her institution as a progressive, innovative correctional system sensitive to social needs and values and flexible enough to change and improve along with society.

References

Alexander, M. E. (1960). Correction at the crossroads. *Crime and Delinquency*, 6:348.

Birnhaum, N. A. (1960). The right to treatment. *ABA Journal*, 46:499.

Bowker, L. (1983). Prisons: Problems and prospects. In Sanford Kadish (Ed.), *Encyclopedia of criminal justice.* New York: The Free Press.

Bureau of Statistics. (1981). *Measuring Crime.* Washington, DC: U.S. Government Printing Office.

Cressey, D. R. (1968). Sources of resistance to innovation in corrections. In *Offenders as a correctional manpower resource.* Washington, DC: Joint Commission on Correctional Manpower and Training, June.

Feldman, R. A., et al. (1972). Treating delinquents in traditional agencies. *Social Work,* 17:73.

Glaser, Daniel. (1971). Five practical research suggestions for correctional administrators. *Crime and Delinquency,* 17(1):32–40.

Innes, C. (1997). Present public opinion in the United States toward punishment and corrections. In J. Marquart and J. Sorensen, eds. *Correctional contexts.* Los Angeles: Roxbury Publishing Co.

Irwin, J. (1980). *Prisons of turmoil.* Boston: Little, Brown.

Irwin, J. and Austin, J. (1997). It's about time: America's imprisonment binge. In J. Marquart and J. Sorensen, eds. *Correctional contexts.* Los Angeles: Roxbury Publishing Co.

Kappeler, V. E. and Potter, G. W. (2005). *The mythology of crime and criminal justice,* 4th ed. Long Grove, IL: Waveland Press.

Marshall, I. H. (1981). Correctional treatment processes: Rehabilitation reconsidered. In R. R. Roberg and V. J. Webb (Eds.), *Critical issues in corrections: Problems, trends, and prospects.* St. Paul: West Publishing Co.

Martinson, R. (1980). What works? Questions and answers about prison reform. In D. M. Petersen and C. W. Thomas (Eds.), *Corrections: Problems and prospects,* 2nd ed. Englewood Cliffs, NJ: Prentice-Hall.

National Advisory Commission on Criminal Justice Standards and Goals. (1973). *Corrections.* Washington, DC: U.S. Government Printing Office.

Quinn, J. F. (2003). *Corrections: A concise introduction,* 2nd ed. Long Grove, IL: Waveland Press.

Roberts, A. R. (1976). Police social workers: A history. *Social Work,* 21:295.

Schwartz, M. and Travis, L. (1997). *Corrections: An issues approach.* Cincinnati: Anderson Publishing Co.

Thomas, C. W. and J. R. Hepburn. (1983). *Crime, criminal law, and criminology.* Dubuque, IA: William C. Brown, Co.

Whitehead, J. T., Pollock, J. and Braswell, M. (2004). *Exploring corrections.* Cincinnati: LexisNexis/Anderson.

CASE 1

Prison Sexuality

You have been superintendent of the state adult correctional facility for six months. Having worked in the field of corrections for over ten years, you have developed quite a list of improvements you would like to implement. These changes include a number of areas in security and treatment.

You can remember when you started out your correctional career as a security officer. After six years of service you were promoted to a security supervisor. Years later you transferred into the counseling department as a Counselor III. Your transfer coincided with your graduation from a nearby university, which you had been attending part-time for a number of years. With your newly earned master's degree in correctional counseling, you attempted to strengthen your institution's treatment program, particularly in the area of crisis intervention, and had achieved some degree of success with your efforts. In your most recent position, you served successfully as an assistant superintendent at a smaller medium-security institution.

Currently, as superintendent, you have methodically worked through your list of improvements. It is six months later, and you have come to item number four: "How to deal effectively with the problems of prison sexuality, particularly sexual assault and the rapidly escalating AIDS problem."

Sexual assaults by aggressive older male inmates against younger prisoners have continued to increase at the prison. It is one thing to tolerate homosexual relationships between consenting adults, but quite another to deal with the young and sometimes older victims of homosexual rape. Of all the difficult situations in which you have found yourself as a prison administrator, the most difficult by far have been the times you have had to face the rape victims. Depressed, humiliated, and emotionally torn apart, they looked to you as a correctional administrator for help, and usually there was little solace you could give them. Sure, you could transfer them to another prison or place them in administrative segregation, but that would provide only a partial solution. You could never guarantee them that they would not be attacked again. They knew what the situation was and, as a result, usually refused to identify their assailants out of fear of an even worse attack as retaliation.

There are a number of theories concerning the best way to handle sexual problems in prison. A well-respected colleague of yours isolated all admitted homosexuals in a single cell block. Another superintendent housed all suspected aggressive homosexuals in a special prison camp, and other administrators tried to segregate all potential rape victims from the general inmate population. Each of these approaches has positive and negative qualities, and you are not sure which one is best. Your institution, which was built in the late 1930s, averages between forty and fifty serious sexual assaults each year that are reported or confirmed by correctional officers. Of course, there is no way to know how many assaults actually occur, since many go unreported. You are not sure which approach is most effective, but as prison superintendent you intend to take the lead in developing a strategy to deal with sexual problems in your prison.

As if sexual assaults weren't enough, there is also the AIDS problem. Out of a population of approximately 1500 adult male inmates, 85 have tested positive and of those, five persons appear to be in the later stages of the disease. These five are in a quarantine section of the prison hospital while the other eighty are housed in a special cell block, although they are allowed to work and otherwise interact with the general population. The prison staff is generally somewhat ill at ease regarding the AIDS patients. In fact, four employees have resigned because of their apprehension. Of course the inmates who have similar feelings have no such choice. In fact, you admit to yourself that you personally share their feelings of uneasiness and concern. No one seems to be able to find a cure, and AIDS awareness isn't what it should be. You have asked the prison chaplains to provide some special counseling and support services for the inmates who have AIDS, but they don't seem to know much about the problem either.

You want to make a serious and sustained attempt to effectively address the sexual problems in your prison, but feel somewhat overwhelmed especially with the development of AIDS. Still, you are determined to try.

Questions for Discussion

In this particular case, would a conjugal or furlough program be more feasible? What might be some of the advantages and disadvantages of each? What are some ways in which you can include security staff members in a comprehensive rape-prevention and treatment program? What about AIDS education, including outside organizations to provide information and services?

Progressive Administration, Punitive Community

Memo

TO: Assistant Superintendent, Joan White

FROM: Superintendent Ralph Harris

RE: Complaints of Concerned Citizens Committee

Please forward to me, within 48 hours of your meeting on June 6th with the committee, your assessment of their concerns and plan for addressing them. Needless to say, we don't want this thing to snowball.

June 6th was yesterday, the report to the superintendent is due tomorrow, and you still aren't sure what to recommend. The Concerned Citizens Committee, or CCC as they like to refer to themselves, is a group of about 100 men and women who want action regarding the imprisonment and punishment of people they refer to as "dangerous individuals." The committee has grown by about 25 members a week since an escape occurred four weeks ago when a local farmer's truck was stolen. The escapee was captured within five days and the truck was returned to the owner, undamaged. Still, fear and panic had been the response of this small rural community of 3,000 people. They overlooked the economic advantages of the new 1,000-bed facility located in their economically depressed county and instead focused on, as they put it in the meeting, "the killers and rapists wasting taxpayers' dollars in an air-conditioned country club." None of the committee had actually visited the new prison, although one person claimed she had a cousin who was fired after two weeks on the job because he wouldn't cater to the wishes of the inmates.

The meeting had been very emotional, and you had to bear the brunt of their anxiety and anger concerning what they imagined rather than knew about the running of the prison and its occupants. You had to listen patiently to such expressions as: "Why are you giving convicts a free education when I have to pay for my children's college?"; "If you ask me, you ought to execute the whole bunch of them and save everybody a lot of trouble"; and "We are going to get the governor to close that place down before somebody gets out of there and rapes or kills our wives and children."

Your being a female corrections administrator didn't help matters any. You couldn't help but notice the disapproving looks of the women who attended the meeting. In fact, you overheard one of them comment to a friend, "Why didn't she choose to be a teacher or a nurse? Working in a prison is no place for a lady." As if that weren't bad enough, when you left the meeting, a middle-aged man said to you with a sly grin on his face, "So you like to be around dangerous men?" You didn't respond to him, but if looks could kill. . . . A follow-up meeting had been scheduled in two weeks, and now you are faced with presenting a report and recommendations to Superintendent Harris. The situation seems pretty hopeless, but something has to be done. Public relations are important, but sometimes public ignorance and fear is hard to overcome. This situation is proving to be a big test for you personally and professionally. You hope you can pass it.

Questions for Discussion

What do you think are some reasons why members of the community feel the way they do about the prison? What kinds of factors contribute to the development of such attitudes? What can you do to address the negative attitudes of the committee? As a female corrections administrator, how does your being a woman influence the concerned citizens? Are there ways you can use the fact that you are a woman to your advantage?

CASE 3

Too Little Supervision or an Unfortunate Incident?

The county jail can accommodate prisoners in a large holding cell called the "Bull Pen." There are also eight other cells designed to accommodate two persons each. Women and juveniles are taken to the next county to a regional jail serving the surrounding four counties. On Saturday nights the jail is usually full with the same repeat drunks and hell-raisers. In addition, there are usually one or two dangerous felons awaiting transport to the state penitentiary, two or three indicted for felonies awaiting trial for offenses ranging from murder to fraud, and some misdemeanants who are serving out their time as well as one or two pretrial detainees who can not make bail. Three deputies are assigned to oversee the jail, two during the day, and one at night. The one working the night shift also helps the dispatcher with in-processing and handles the radio in the dispatcher's absence. The facility is about twenty-five years old and takes on the characteristics of a "zoo" when it is full. Nevertheless, it is solid and well built, and there has never been a breakout. The population averages about twenty-one, day in and day out. You, as the chief county correctional officer, are usually on the day shift. You stay busy with booking, inventory, release, court appearances, overseeing visits, mail delivery, and phone calls. When one of your correctional officers is sick or on vacation, a deputy from the patrol division may be called in by the sheriff to help as needed. This Sunday you are working the graveyard shift for an officer who is taking some vacation time.

A deputy from the patrol division brought in a twenty-year-old male, who attended a local university, for drunk driving. The young man, obviously drunk and sick, was found in his car on the side of the road near the state park where a rock band had been in concert that day. James Bright was from a nearby town and had no previous record. He was melancholy, contrite, and drunk. It was 2 AM when you locked Bright up in a vacant cell after taking his personal property. There is a clear view down the aisle from the desk at the reception counter where the officer in charge can see and hear what is going on. You can shut the steel door to the aisle if necessary, but usually it is open in compliance with jail operating procedure. The jail operating procedure also specified: "periodic cell checks at irregular intervals, but not less than one an hour apart."

Aside from some snoring and moaning, the jail cells seemed quiet. You checked all the offense reports and determined who will be getting out in the morning. The sheriff wanted them out before breakfast, if possible, so he can save on meal costs. You made a couple of phone calls and the radio started popping. The highway patrol had a driver's license checkpoint in the next county, and some motorists were turning off just before the checkpoint and heading for a bypass route in your county. The radio operator turned rather pale. It seemed his wife was caught at the checkpoint with someone in the car when she was supposed to be home. The operator asked you to handle dispatch for an hour while he checked out the situation with his wife. He left before you had a chance to respond to his request. The night passed and the radio operator eventually returned in a foul mood.

It was 6 AM when you took a walk down the aisle and started calling the names of people to be released. You called for James Bright and no one answered. You called again; no answer. When you got to Bright's cell to awaken him, he appeared to have slipped off his bunk and seemed to be asleep on the floor. You opened the cell door and were shocked to see that Bright had made a noose from his shoelaces and tightened it around his neck. He had tied the other end to the bunk rail and laid down with the weight of his head and shoulders tightening the noose until he passed out. He had apparently died from strangulation. You called for the radio operator to summon the fire department's rescue truck while you untied the noose and began pounding on his chest. Mouth-to-mouth resuscitation was out of the question since there were no resuscitation kits, and you were not about to touch this man's mouth with his eyes wide open and tongue hanging out. In addition, you really did not know much about CPR, having only tried it once when you were in the Law Enforcement Training Academy. The cool body temperature indicated there was little you could do to help anyway.

The sheriff viewed the scene and asked the dreaded question, "When did you check him last? Did you write it down in your log?"

"Sheriff," you respond. "I checked all of them two or three times after I booked him in at 2 AM; he looked all right to me. I did have to watch the radio for an hour or two while Jimmy got his wife from the highway patrol road block. There wasn't a sound coming from that cell that would make me the least bit suspicious."

The sheriff looked around the jail. The rest of the prisoners were restless, hanging on the cell bars. One shouted, "Sheriff, I want out of here! It ain't safe here. Somebody must have killed that kid. You know you can't hang yourself off no bed!"

"Shut up," responded the sheriff. He was beginning to see a potential problem.

After the coroner had finished his fact gathering and estimating the time of death, it was apparent that you had missed one, maybe two checks. Although you had recorded all the checks on the log, the neat row of checks and times looked like they were all recorded at the same time, a not-unheard-of practice by custodial personnel at the end of the night shift. The good news, if there was any, was that the death was probably a suicide.

The family complained and the FBI came to investigate. You were censured for untying the ligature rather than cutting it, and for falsifying the log of cell checks. This fact was easily developed from interviewing prisoners in the adjacent cells.

It was not 100% proven that Bright was not murdered, but the preponderance of evidence pointed to suicide. The lawsuit asked for unspecified damages and alleged that the sheriff failed to properly train his jail staff, failed to provide proper supervision of the jail when the radio operator was out, and failed to provide a safe environment for his prisoners. Particularly, the suit alleged that the correctional officers should have known Bright was a suicide risk. He was a white, twenty-year-old male, a first offender and remorseful. Further, the failure of the correctional officer to remove Bright's long shoe strings was a negligent act indicative of the lack of training and supervision contributing materially to the absence of a safe environment in the jail. Your CPR experience was not discussed.

After six months of legal expenses, the county's lawyers recommended a settlement offer of $300,000 with an initial offer of $150,000. The sheriff was told to do something to improve his jail operation. The sheriff was also asked to provide the county commissioners with a priority list of improvements to be made in the jail, and cost estimates. The commissioners may have held the sheriff responsible for the jail's operation, but as the chief correctional officer, he held you responsible. Of course, after this, you might not be chief correctional officer for long. The sheriff passed the commissioners' request on to you with a curt reply that he wants the situation "cleaned up" by the end of the working day.

Questions for Discussion

Successful management at any level of corrections requires constant and diligent supervision. The courts have shown a willingness to hold state and local jurisdictions responsible for assuring constitutional standards in correctional facilities. What would be on your list of needs to improve supervision and safety within the jail, and the training of operating personnel? What particular item would be your first priority, and why? How about the chief correctional officer? What should be done about him?

CASE 4

Managing a Women's Prison

You are the new superintendent at the state adult women's prison. No one believed you would continue working toward a career in correctional administration. Even your husband, a physician, from time to time doubted the value of your efforts. You persevered, and now, in your mid-thirties and after nine years of marriage, a career, and two children, you have been appointed superintendent.

After your first tour of the institution, you were somewhat disheartened. The drab green paint was peeling off the walls. The prison library consisted of sixty or so books and a ragged set of encyclopedias. The recreation room was poorly stocked with damaged equipment from the men's prison. The faces of the women pretty much reflected their environment and the winter season—depressed.

Your first objective was to remodel the facility, if painting the walls and repairing the heating system could be considered remodeling. In any event, two coats of paint and a new heating system later, the place at least looked more cheerful.

The administrative problems facing you are numerous and immense. The prison needs increased treatment, vocational, and educational programs; improved health care; additional facility renovations and additions; improvement in food preparation and quality; more effective prison security; and additional correctional personnel. Correcting the deficiencies in the women's prison would require not only sophisticated management skills, but a substantially increased operating budget as well. The state commissioner's initial response to your budget request was not very supportive. Since women inmates comprise only 10% of the state's incarcerated adult offenders, the commissioner was reluctant to allocate funds he felt could be better utilized elsewhere.

You could not help feeling that his reluctance stems at least in part from his being a man; you feel that he does not give the

204

women's prison the consideration it deserves because he is not aware of the needs of women. How could a man fully understand the special needs of female offenders? Somehow you have to help him become more aware of the female offender. Even if you can gain some budget increases, that probably will not be enough. Community resources may also be available if you can motivate local business and civic leaders. Being a female superintendent of a women's prison has proven to be as much of a challenge as you thought it would. Changes need to be made. You have the will and now must find the way.

Questions for Discussion

What are some ways that you, as the new superintendent of the women's prison, could encourage support for needed changes? Perhaps the state commissioner might be invited to visit the institution and talk to a group of female inmates. Could you write prominent women who were civic leaders and in state government to visit the prison and discuss issues and possible solutions?

CASE 5

Where Do You Begin?

You accepted the governor's appointment to be commissioner of the Department of Corrections knowing that some very difficult decisions were looming regarding budget issues. You will also be confronting questions about the department's overall performance, since the governor made the Department of Corrections a very high-profile issue during his campaign.

Now the governor has met with you and has directed that $35 million be cut from the department's budget. You try to warn the governor that such a massive budget reduction will have catastrophic consequences for the department. The governor further instructs you to reorganize, downsize, and force as many senior, higher-paid staff to retire as possible. You must have a draft proposal to him within 30 days. As a matter of protocol, you feel obliged to inform the chairmen of your House and Senate Corrections Committees of the pending budget cuts that you will soon be required to make. Both chairmen are angered by the governor's directive to you, especially since he has not discussed it with them. There is going to be conflict between the governor and the legislature concerning the budget cuts, and you feel like you are caught in the middle.

No matter where you cut an already lean budget, morale will plummet among inmate and staff alike, making prison environments more unstable. Can technology in such areas as surveillance compensate for reductions in correctional officer staff positions? What about volunteer chaplains to cover the responsibilities of the two staff chaplains? Could food services absorb some of the budget reductions? You could ally yourself with House and Senate legislators, but if you lose, you might be fired. Or you could resign rather than be the "hatchet man" for the governor.

Questions for Discussion

You must examine every facet of your department's operations to determine where and how to most effectively achieve the necessary reductions. Where do you begin? How do you reassure the legislature and the citizenry that public safety will not be compromised by cuts to the Department of Corrections? Is such reassurance even possible? What action will you take?

The Execution Protocol

You have been a warden for more than a decade, serving at several different institutions. Most recently, you were transferred to the state's highest-security prison which houses, among other things, Death Row. Although you have not carried out any executions since becoming a warden, you did serve on an execution team while a deputy warden. During that experience you learned a lot about human nature and behavior, especially when it came to selecting prison staff to serve on the execution team.

Just a week ago you were served with a death warrant for prisoner Clyde Jones, who has been on the row for nearly fifteen years. The attorney general advises you that barring any unforeseen last minute legal problems, the execution will be "a go." You immediately begin addressing the many aspects of the execution "protocol" that must be done in preparation for the execution. The biggest of those is the appointment of prison staff to various roles on the execution team. This is an extremely delicate and sensitive task. You want staff who are professional and reliable, but who also have a sense of humanness and compassion about carrying out their duties. You want everything to go off without a hitch, no room for human error or equipment malfunction.

Questions for Discussion

How do you go about filling out your execution team? What precautions should you take in selecting specific staff members for the execution team?

CASE 7

If It's Not Broken . . .

You have been the warden at the Stateline Prison for some twenty years. Recently, a new commissioner of corrections, Dr. Sally Given, was appointed by the governor. While she is well qualified and very experienced, you have been uncomfortable with the number of policy decisions she has made so soon after her appointment. Because she came to the agency from another region of the country, in your opinion she is unfamiliar with the particular nuances and traditions of the Department of Corrections. You have tried, in a respectful manner, to counsel her against making changes simply for the sake of change.

Most recently, she has told you that she intends to reorganize and update the inmate classification system so that fewer long-term offenders will be in trustee positions. You attempt to discuss the ramifications of her plan with the commissioner, pointing out that the present system has worked well and that it was subjected to review just two years ago. You also note that in your two decades as warden there has never been a major incident involving trustee inmates. However, your arguments are to no avail. Dr. Given's last words before hanging up are, "It's time for Stateline Prison to join the twenty-first century."

Questions for Discussion

You do not wish to be viewed by the commissioner as an obstructionist. You want to be a team player, yet you feel very strongly that the present system works quite effectively and should not be fixed if it's not broken. What, if anything, can you do?